Miracle IN BORNEO

By Norma R. Youngberg

Illustrated by Harold W. Munson

TEACH Services, Inc.
PUBLISHING
www.TEACHServices.com • (800) 367-1844

World rights reserved. This book or any portion thereof may not be copied or reproduced in any form or manner whatever, except as provided by law, without the written permission of the publisher, except by a reviewer who may quote brief passages in a review.

The author assumes full responsibility for the accuracy of all facts and quotations as cited in this book. The opinions expressed in this book are the author's personal views and interpretations, and do not necessarily reflect those of the publisher.

This book is provided with the understanding that the publisher is not engaged in giving spiritual, legal, medical, or other professional advice. If authoritative advice is needed, the reader should seek the counsel of a competent professional.

Copyright © 2005 TEACH Services, Inc.
ISBN-13: 978-1-57258-354-2 (Paperback)
Library of Congress Control Number: 2005928603

CONTENTS

1.	A Charm for Cherawa	7
2.	Stricken Village	20
3.	The Naga Makes Medicine	35
4.	Under the Ban	48
5.	A Song in the River	61
6.	The Eater of Souls	75
7.	Lost—One Small Galeega	89
8.	One New Skin—What Price?	102
9.	The Believers	109
10.	The Medicine House	124
11.	Tercoop or Heaven	136
12.	Peekew—His Victory	151
13.	Jesus Is My Galeega	164

AUTHOR'S PREFACE

This book has been written to describe the transformation wrought on Tatau River by Christian teachers.

Another aim of this book is to emphasize the important work of the native evangelist. Few realize how much the expansion of gospel work in foreign lands depends on teachers such as Deckie. There are hundreds of such humble souls, whose devotion and courage constitute the front line of advance against heathenism.

I have purposely kept the missionary and his family in the background where they belong.

It is my earnest prayer that this little story may lead many to a greater appreciation of their fellow believers in the island of Borneo, and to a new reliance on the God who must work as great a miracle to save a soul in America as on Tatau River.

N. R. Y.

There was a mutual feeling of admiration between Cherawa and her father, Rayang, who was the most capable chief in the district.

CHAPTER ONE

A CHARM FOR CHERAWA

"COME, Little One, bring me another paddle." Chief Rayang stood on the log wharf just below his village and motioned his young daughter up the notched log to the long house.

Cherawa ran lightly up the crude ladder and returned with the paddle in her hand. At the top of the ladder she paused to look down with great pride at the chief, her father. He was a handsome man in the prime of life. His black hair was wound into a long knot on the back of his head, and the forelock was cut to make a fringe low on his forehead. His eyes were keen and black. He wore a new red loincloth and heavy earrings that pulled the split lobes of his ears down almost to his shoulders.

Up and down the river he was known and respected as the most capable chief of that part of Borneo; but to his daughter, Cherawa, he was the embodiment of every perfection. No father was ever more tenderly loved. She looked him over with a warm surge of joy in her heart, then hurried down the ladder of notched log and placed the paddle in his hand.

"Where are we going, Father?" Cherawa questioned as she took her place in the prow of the dugout canoe.

Chief Rayang settled himself in the stern of the small boat before answering. He leaned forward and examined the collection of knives and spears that lay between them in the canoe. Satisfying himself that all was in order, he loosed the dugout from its mooring at the log wharf and guided it out into the broad, swift river. Then, at last, he remembered that Cherawa had asked him a question.

"Mapang was hunting up on Sungi Sap yesterday. He thinks he saw a Naga there. I must go and see."

"Oh, yes, I heard the mother of Mapang telling about it. It was just getting dark. Mapang was coming home with a deer in his canoe. The Naga was resting on the river bank. Its skin was shining like the rainbow. It was long, oh, very long, ten times as long as this canoe. It had two great horns on its head, and its eyes were above its horns. It looked at Mapang—" Cherawa broke off her gay chatter about the Naga, shivered, and was quiet.

After a thoughtful pause Rayang spoke again:

"We have heard about the great Naga for years. It is the king of dragons; and when it appears to men, it always has an important meaning. It may mean that evil is coming to this river, or it might mean that great good is coming."

"Did you ever see a Naga, Father?" Cherawa plied her small paddle with diligence.

"No, child, I can't say for certain that I ever saw one. Once for two evenings the clouds at sunset cradled a dark form like a giant serpent. The old men of the village said it was the great Naga and that evil would certainly come to the river. I was a small boy then, but I remember it well."

"Did it really look like a serpent?" Cherawa began to shiver again.

"Well, I can't say that it looked so to me, but soon after that the great sickness came to the river. Whole villages died of it in a few days. Then everyone remembered the Naga in the sunset. They said it was a warning."

Cherawa felt her heart beating fast, but it was broad daylight. The morning was still young. A Naga by daylight or in open sunshine would certainly not be so terrifying as a Naga in the sunset or seen by night.

Chief Rayang guided the little boat into the mouth of Sungi Sap. It was not far down river from the home village. It was much too close for comfort.

Sungi Sap was a tributary of the Tatau; it was one of the larger streams that fed that great river. The banks were far enough apart so Cherawa had no immediate fear that the Naga might spring from the bank and engulf the canoe. However, she observed with satisfaction that her father kept the boat in midstream.

The chief paddled more slowly now and kept his keen eyes fixed on the left bank of the river. The stream was bordered with heavy jungle except for a few swampy places where the tall lalang grass grew rank along the shore.

An object on a jutting sand bar arrested his attention. They had now come far up the stream, much farther than Mapang had come. Rayang knew that the small, dark thing on the sand bar was not a Naga. Most people would not have seen it at all, but to the sharp eyes of the chief it was something to be investigated. He swung the boat in toward the sand bar, grabbed his spear, and knelt beside the body of a dead monkey. Cherawa was at his side.

"This is the first time in my life that I ever found a dead monkey," Rayang informed Cherawa. "It must have died of some sickness. The crabs and ants have been busy with it."

Rayang turned the carcass over and looked at it with keen interest. Then with his spear he laid open the belly of the monkey. Cherawa drew back and held her

Finding the greatest of charms, Cherawa's father leaped with joy.

nose. Rayang deftly laid the internal organs bare, picked up the liver, and examined it with great care. He felt it all over, cut into it several times, and extracted a small, irregular stone about the size of the end of his thumb. He knelt at the edge of the sand bar and washed the stone in the river. Then he held out his hand to Cherawa. She looked with fascinated interest at the stone.

"It is a galeega! It is a galeega!" Cherawa had seldom seen her father so excited. He leaped into the air brandishing his spear. He whooped and shouted with joy. Then dropping to a squatting position, he again stretched out his hand with the galeega resting in it.

"Look, child, this is wonderful luck! I have heard my grandfather say that if one ever finds a dead monkey in the forest, it is possible the liver of the animal may contain a galeega." He was trembling with excitement.

"Is it a charm, my Father?" Cherawa bent to examine the stone with new interest.

"It is the greatest charm known to our witch doctors," Rayang explained; "there is not one on this river now. A few years ago, when you were a baby, the old witch doctor had a small one. It was his most valuable possession."

"What became of it when he died?"

"The old man knew he was going to die. He had the cough, and the blood came in his throat for several months. Right at the last he took his most precious charms and buried them in some secret place in the jungle. When his family looked over his things after he had been taken to the burial tree, the galeega was gone. They have searched for it ever since, but who could find a secret burial place in the forest?" Rayang shook his head.

"Peekew doesn't have a galeega then, I guess." Cherawa regarded the stone with growing wonder. "Peekew is a powerful witch doctor, too."

"Peekew is the most powerful witch doctor on this river," Rayang agreed, "but he has no galeega. He would give all his possessions to have this one, I am sure; but I don't intend for him to know anything about it. The spirits have given it to us, and we will keep it. It shall be for you, my Cherawa. You are the daughter of Rayang, the chief."

"Oh, Father!" Cherawa jumped to her feet in wild excitement. "For me? Can I wear it?"

"Yes, we will make you a new necklace. You can wear it all the time. It will protect you from all danger and keep you well. It will bring you a good husband. Oh, it will do wonderful things for you!" The chief had risen and held the precious charm high above his head. "It will give you great power. You will be able

Cherawa and her father discussed the great things the charm would do.

to touch the bodies of sick people with the galeega, and their pain will leave them. You will be able to get whatever you want with the galeega."

"Father," Cherawa said as she caught his hand and pulled him toward the carcass of the dead monkey, "let us take the monkey's teeth for my necklace. Is it not a good-luck monkey?"

"Good idea!" exclaimed Rayang as he knelt again beside the carcass. He broke out all the teeth, and after washing them in the river, tied them, together with the galeega, in the end of his new red loincloth. After this he dragged the monkey to the river's edge and pushed it in. Father and daughter stood watching it until the swift stream carried it round a curve and out of sight. Then they entered their canoe.

Before casting off from their mooring place, they ate their simple lunch. Rayang produced two balls of rice, wrapped in banana leaf, and offered one to his daughter. In a matter of a few minutes they finished, and Rayang untied the boat. He let it drift down the stream, guiding it with dexterous motions of his guide paddle. The discovery of the galeega had almost banished thoughts of the Naga from their minds. Still, Rayang kept to the middle of the stream.

Then the chief saw it! A startled cry burst from his lips. He recognized it by the two large branching horns. It lay close to the bank of the river. It was a very large serpent, and its face was turned toward the two rowers in the dugout.

Neither Rayang nor his daughter had any notion of stopping to investigate this new wonder. Both of them laid to their oars, and neither breathed or spoke until they had rounded the next curve of the stream.

"Was it really the Naga?" Cherawa could hold her question no longer.

"It must be!" Rayang caught his breath and rested a little on his paddle. "It must be! The horns are a sure sign."

"Do you think it means evil will come to this river?" His daughter pressed him for an answer.

"I don't know. Oh, I don't know!" Rayang looked with wild eyes up to the blue noon heavens, down to the blue water, and yonder to the tall green jungle; but he found no answer to the question his daughter had put into words.

"I think this is an enchanted river." Cherawa smiled at last. "I think since we found the galeega, it must mean good fortune. I think something very good is going to happen." She looked into her father's troubled face.

"You are only thirteen years old, my child; you know little of good or evil fortune. Evil can come to a whole tribe in the form of war or sickness. But what good can come to this river?"

"Everyone could have a wonderful rice crop this year, and the men might all have good fishing and hunting." Cherawa tried to think what would really be good fortune for the river.

"I hope you are right, Little One," Rayang said as his eyes rested with affection on his daughter. "I do hope you are right. Anyhow, the galeega is the most powerful charm in the world. You will always have that, so it should be good fortune for you." With this he brightened perceptibly and bent again to his rowing.

They had now reached the mouth of the Sungi Sap, and just before turning the canoe into the swift current of the larger river, they rested a little.

The hot sun shone down on them with tropical fury. Rayang had loosened his long hair, and it hung over his perspiring back like a mantle. Cherawa had put on her palm-leaf hat, which was cone-shaped and cool, but even these gestures could not much alleviate the discomfort of the heat; for both the chief and his daughter were covered from head to foot with skin ringworm. As they rested, they scratched and scratched. Little trickles of blood followed their fingers down their brown arms and legs. The ringworm always itched, especially at night and out in the hot sun. Neither the chief nor his daughter had ever known a good night's rest. Both had been infected with the ringworm from babyhood. Neither could remember anything different. Everyone on the river had long ceased to regard it as anything but normal. Long ago they had stopped pointing out the old man who had brought the scourge to the river. He was very old now and seldom left the long house.

As Rayang turned the small craft into the larger stream, he sensed some change in the river. At first he could not define the feeling or see what caused it. Then, as his keen vision swept both banks of the Tatau, he saw it. A large boat was tied to a single floating log moored to the shore opposite his own village of Rayang and a little downstream. It was at the mouth of Nyala Creek where a spot of rich swampland was interrupted by a beautiful green hill rising a hundred feet above the water. Close to the river's edge was a plot of level ground which the chief of Sawa Village had cleared for a rice field the year before.

Rayang and Cherawa both saw the boat. It was painted white and had two portholes like eyes at its prow. It had some black marks on its side, but these were without meaning to the chief and his daughter. It was too large a craft to be propelled by paddles. It must have one of those throbbing, pounding things in it that made it go. Cherawa had seen such a boat at Tatau Fort.

"What is it, my Father?" Cherawa whispered the question, although they were still some distance down the stream, and no person was visible from the boat. "I never saw it before," admitted the chief. "We will go and see what it is." So saying, he guided the canoe toward the larger boat, and soon the dugout was laid alongside the launch. He stood up in the canoe and looked over the prow of the larger boat. It was hollow inside, with two bunks running lengthwise and curved to fit the contour of the launch. A deck of heavy planking covered the front two thirds of its length. Back of this a window looked out over the deck, and a wheel was sheltered there, also a seat for the master of the craft.

Down below the seat was a black creature, which looked dead all right, but Rayang assured his daughter that it could come to life fast enough when its master appeared. It had a strong heart, one that could be felt beating when the animal was not asleep. He put out his hand and touched it.

"Feel of it, Little One," he said; "you see it is warm."

Cherawa laid her small, brown hand against the hard skin of the creature. Sure enough, it was quite warm. "It has the fever, my Father," she exclaimed with understanding. "But of course it is a hot day."

Since there was no one about and the launch had been thoroughly investigated, Rayang turned homeward across the river.

CHAPTER TWO

STRICKEN VILLAGE

IT was midafternoon when Chief Rayang again made his dugout fast to his home wharf. Two men loitered there awaiting his return. Peekew and Mapang searched the face of the chief as he stepped from his boat, and they directed questioning glances at Cherawa. It was evident to the shrewd eyes of both that something unusual had happened to the chief and his daughter. Peekew and Mapang had seen the canoe of the chief alongside the white launch. That might have accounted for the evident agitation in Rayang's manner.

"Did you see the Naga?" Mapang asked as he spat a wad of betel nut into the river.

"We saw it," Rayang stated with naked simplicity. Then turning to Peekew, he said, "Does it mean good or evil? It must mean something!"

Peekew's small, black eyes peered at the chief

from under his heavy bob of black hair. His restless hands fondled the handle of a knife at his belt. He did not answer at once, and when he did, it was in a voice so low and musical that one could never get over being surprised. Peekew was a great witch doctor, feared and respected far and near. He was powerful and could be cruel, but his voice was the sweetest the Ibans had ever heard.

"Perhaps we cannot tell about that at once," Peekew began; "we must entreat the spirits with offerings and devotions to find out such a secret. But, as you say, it must mean something."

"We have no time for devotions today." Mapang spoke with more than his usual energy. "You see that boat moored yonder? There are three men with it. They have asked to stay at this long house tonight." Mapang gestured with both hands to show that he felt this placed a great responsibility on Chief Rayang.

"But what sort of men are they?" Rayang asked. "Are they from the government? Is it about the taxes they come?"

"There is a Chinese and an Iban, or at least he looks like an Iban, and he speaks our language. Then there is a white tuan." Mapang counted them off on his fingers. "They say they are going to build a village over there—well, not a long house like this, but they intend to build a place to live."

Chief Rayang squatted down on the wharf and drew out his betel nut. With grave deliberation he rolled the Areca nut and lime into the ciri leaf and began chewing. His two companions did likewise. Now they were in proper condition to consider this astounding news.

Cherawa saw that the deliberations were likely to take a long time, so she slipped past the men and ran up the notched log into the village. The women would be more talkative.

She found her own mother, Dawee, the center of an excited group of women, chattering and babbling in great confusion.

"The white tuan is a great witch doctor," said Treesa, their nearest neighbor on the left. "He has powerful medicine. He can make lazy men work. He can make barren women have children. He can make new teeth grow after the rotten ones have fallen out. He can turn white hair black. I heard the Chinese at Tatau Fort telling about that tuan."

Treesa sat cross-legged on the floor with a tiny baby in her arms. Another baby, a year or so older, clung to her short skirt. Treesa's heavy hair hung loose and lay in waves along the bamboo floor. Her large, dark eyes had a peculiar quality. It always seemed to Cherawa that Treesa was looking through or beyond whatever she fixed her eyes upon. Treesa was a devotee of the spirits. She was interested in medicine of all kinds and in other peculiar things. Often in the night she went to a secret meeting place to talk with her familiar spirit. From these conferences deep in the jungle she frequently brought back messages to her fellow villagers. "You are not to go to your rice field today," she would tell some householder as he was about to step into his canoe; "the spirits warn you."

No villager was so foolish as to disregard such a communication from the spirit world. The rice crop might waste in the field; the long-awaited fruit might rot on the trees; but no spirit message was disobeyed, and no evil omen went unregarded.

"But what will happen if a white witch doctor comes to live on this river?" Dawee inquired of the group. "It will be interesting to see whether the Iban medicine men are as clever as the white tuan."

"I think it will be a good thing," spoke another woman; "the more medicine the better, I say. Of course you all know that if we could eat enough medicine, none of us would ever be sick or have any bad luck."

"That white tuan will have some good liquor too, I'm sure," said another. "All the white tuans have it. If we can just get some of that, what fine devil dances we can have! I think it is a good thing."

Cherawa listened but said nothing. In her heart she guarded a mighty secret. She had the galeega. It was the most powerful medicine charm known to man. Let white men, brown men, and yellow men come; she was safe from their charms because of the galeega.

Cherawa's brother, Chendang, had been squatting near the group of women. Now he detached himself and joined his sister.

"Did you see the Naga?" he whispered. Cherawa drew him away to the open veranda, far from the cluster of chattering women.

"Yes, I saw it," she said. "It was just as Mapang told us; it had great horns, and its eyes were above its horns, and it was long—oh, very long—and it lay on the river bank."

Chendang shuddered. "I would like to see it," he said with bravado.

"Well, once is enough for me," Cherawa shrugged. "It may be a good omen; I hope it is, but I don't want to see the Naga any more. It reminds me too much of the time I was lost in the jungle and found the big snake in the bamboo."

"That was a good omen," Chendang laughed. "They found you that day when the snake came to life, and they brought home so much snake meat that we had a great feast. Maybe the Naga will bring us good luck too."

Chief Rayang and his two advisers came up the ladder into the long house. Cherawa understood that

Peekew would go himself on the morrow to interview His Dragon Highness. He would undertake to learn something of the Naga's intentions.

From their talk Cherawa also knew that the three strangers in the white boat would be welcomed to their village that evening.

Mapang went into his door and came out with his paddle. He had been delegated to act as the chief's messenger to inform the three strangers that the great Chief Rayang would extend them hospitality.

Cherawa and Chendang stood on the high open veranda of the long house and watched Mapang's boat cross the river. The two children never shifted their position until they heard the put-put of the launch sound faintly across the river. The white boat swung out into the stream heading for their own log wharf. As it drew nearer, they could see Mapang's canoe being trailed by the launch. Mapang was aboard the larger boat and held his little dugout by a stout rattan.

Chendang jumped up and down and clapped his hands. "Oh, I would like to ride on that white boat! See, it goes by itself! How fast it comes! What a big wave it pushes before it!"

"It doesn't go by itself," Cherawa informed him; "there is a black animal in the boat that makes it go. It makes that put-put sound when it is awake. It breathes and it is warm."

Cherawa intensely observed the white launch of the three strangers.

"I want to see it! I want to see it!" Chendang was getting more and more excited. So was everyone else in the village. The men and boys scrambled down the notched log to the landing, but the women and smaller children crept into their rooms and quaked.

Cherawa did neither. She stood still at her post of observation. The white launch made fast to the wharf. Mapang leaped off and made his boat fast. Then a small young man climbed out of the launch onto the wharf. Cherawa could see that he was dark-skinned like an Iban, although he was not exactly the same as an Iban. Cherawa was too excited to consider what the difference was. The young man wore long trousers the color of a dead leaf, a shirt of the same material, and a sun helmet of the same brown color. His features were delicate—almost like a girl's—and he was quite young; but the smile that never left his face was so radiant that after Cherawa looked at him for a little while, everything else was forgotten but the smile.

The Chinese man was next off the launch. He had on dark blue trousers and a white shirt open at the throat. He was lean and wiry looking, stooped a little as though he had carried heavy loads for many years; but his face was kind and pleasant. Cherawa thought he might be the same age as her own father.

Then the white man scrambled off the launch. He was much taller than the other two. He was taller than Chief Rayang. He was thin, and although one could see that he belonged to the white people, his skin was tanned almost as brown as that of his companions. His face was homely. His nose was too big and long. His eyes were large and deep-set and gray, the color of the river on a cloudy day. His ears were big, too, and his chin was pointed. Still Cherawa felt strangely drawn to him. There was a peculiar sweetness of expression about his mouth so that although he did not smile often, yet one felt the kindness in him. And when he laughed, as he frequently did, it was a most pleasant sound to hear; and his voice when he spoke was as mellow and melting as Peekew's.

The visitors were brought up into the long house. The young man with the smile assured Chief Rayang that they had brought along food of their own and also their sleeping cots and nets. All they wanted was a place to spread their things, and they would make ready for the night.

The young man was called Deckie. He hurried up and down the notched log fetching bundles from the launch while the Chinese man and the tuan unrolled blankets and set up some strange sleeping platforms on six slender legs. Each one was just right for one person to sleep on. White mosquito curtains were then hung over the sleeping platforms and well tucked in.

Cherawa was so interested in the doings of the

strangers she forgot her supper. She saw the tuan take small objects from their bundles. They looked to Cherawa like generous slices of a well-peeled sapling. She wondered whether they would eat them raw or cook them. While she was considering this, the Chinese man took his pointed pocket knife and punched two holes in the end of one of the queer things. Then he turned it up and poured out a small stream of white fluid into a bright, shining dish. Dawee brought some boiling water, and the Chinese poured it in, too, mixing it all together with a ladle of the same bright material. Then he poured the white fluid out into bright cups, and all three men drank it eagerly. Deckie brought out a package, opened it, and passed it to his two companions. It contained small, square things that looked like thick shavings of light-colored wood. The men ate these with their drink. They seemed to be crisp and easy to chew.

The simple meal was soon over. The night was falling. The visitors went to the wharf for their evening bath and returned clad in light sleeping garments. The men of the village were all waiting, sitting cross-legged in a circle with a faint light from a coconut oil lamp in the middle of the circle. Places had been left for the visitors near Chief Rayang.

It was Deckie who opened the conversation. He addressed the chief with much respect: "Chief Rayang, the government has kindly given us a tract of land directly across the river from your village. We expect to build homes there and live among you. We have brought medicine, and we will have a medicine house where sick people may come and be helped. We will have a house for teaching where your children may come and learn to read and write and to make many useful things."

The chief grunted, but he did not look displeased. It was Mapang who answered the young teacher: "As for living across the river from us, we have no objection. As for your medicine, we have good medicine of our own. Our fathers never learned to read or write, and they did very well, so we see no need of changing our ways."

The smile never left Deckie's face. "All right, then we will just be your neighbors, and you can teach us many things about the jungle. We will ask you to help us with our undertaking. Best of all, we will be good friends."

The tuan had been looking around, and now he saw Cherawa squatting in the shadow of a pile of winnowing baskets. He motioned her to come to him. She was almost afraid to go, but something in the man's kind face drew her to him. He took from a bundle beside him a bright cup such as she had seen the men use at suppertime. Then he took out another and an-

The kind missionary presented Cherawa four shiny cups and four spoons.

other until four cups rested in her hands, nestled one inside another. Then he gave her four spoons of the same hard, shiny material. He held up his hand and counted off four fingers. He nodded with a bright smile and motioned for Cherawa to take them away. She understood that they were a present for her family—one for father, one for mother, one for Chendang, and one for herself. What wonderful good fortune! The galeega had already begun to bring her luck! No one in the village had ever seen such luxury. She carried the presents to Dawee, who had crept out of her room and was watching from the shadows of the veranda.

The conversation among the men lagged. The circle broke up, and the strangers sought their sleeping platforms. No light but moonlight filtered through the far end of the porch where their equipment was spread, but in that pale light Cherawa saw all three of the men kneel for a few moments beside their beds. A hush fell over the scattered watchers. They realized that these men must be holding communion with the spirits or with some object of worship. Then the visitors lay down to rest and tucked their mosquito curtains about them.

Cherawa was fascinated. She could not withdraw. She did not feel sleepy. She heard Treesa whispering to her mother. Then a little group of women gathered around them. Treesa stepped to the cot where the tuan lay, and shook the net a little to attract his attention. "Tuan, I have a severe headache. Do you not have some medicine for headaches?" She held both hands to her head and looked quite miserable.

The tuan understood the gesture and lifted the net. He drew out his bundle from beneath the cot and produced a small white jar. He unwound the end of it and dipped his finger into the contents. He rubbed a little on Treesa's temples, on the back of her neck, and under her nose. Then with his great, strong hands he massaged the muscles in her neck and her temples.

"Ah," said Treesa, much impressed, "this is indeed powerful medicine. My headache is better; in fact I think it is gone. Wonderful! Wonderful!"

The tuan drew himself back into his net and settled himself again for sleep; but another woman crept shyly up and announced that she, too, had a bad headache.

This time a broad smile played round the white man's mouth, but he administered the same remedy as before, and the woman exclaimed with vigor that her headache had also vanished. This time the tuan made no move to retire. He waited in amused silence for the next arrival. At last every woman in the village had been cured of a raging headache by the magic medicine. Last of all Cherawa managed to gather courage to come with her headache to the white man. The medicine was cool and delightful. It had an odor like crushed leaves, sweet and pungent. The touch of the tuan's strong, skillful hands was soothing and refreshing. Soon Cherawa's headache went the way of all the others. She had also experienced the magic of the tuan's medicine. Then the tired man prepared again to rest.

"Tuan, tuan." It was Mapang speaking. "I have a dreadful stomach-ache. Do you not have some powerful medicine for stomachs?"

The white man was up again, and this time he produced a long object the shape of a man's foot, but it was a bag. It was white and seemed to be full of medicine. Joy of joys! What wonderful good fortune! Deckie was up too now and ordered Mapang to bring a coconut shell full of water. The tuan measured a very large spoonful of the medicine, mixed it with the water in the coconut shell, and told Mapang to drink it all. He did so, making a wry face but ending with a beaming smile. "Ah, wonderful!" he exclaimed. "My stomach-ache is all gone. The tuan's medicine is powerful indeed."

"What did it taste like, Mapang?" asked Peekew.

"Oh, it was wonderful! It tasted salty and sharp and bitter all together, but when I washed it down with water, it tasted sweet at the last."

"Tuan, please, tuan, I have a bad stomach-ache, too." Peekew was going to try the medicine himself.

Then all the men had stomach-aches.

CHAPTER THREE

THE NAGA MAKES MEDICINE

"MY FATHER, how shall we make the galeega a part of the necklace?" Cherawa squatted beside her father on the outer veranda of the long house. She was watching with delighted interest the polishing of the monkey teeth and the dexterous use Rayang was making of a fine drill as he bored a hole in each one so they might be strung on a stout leather thong.

Rayang reached for the tail of his loincloth and untied a rather large knot in the red cotton. He held out the tusk of a wild pig for Cherawa to see. It was a small tusk, not heavy, but shapely and well polished.

"Look, Little One," he said as he held the tusk affectionately in both hands; "we will make a hollow in the boar's tusk and fasten the galeega safely inside. Then it will be secure. Also no one will know the secret of your charm."

"Peekew will surely find out about the galeega," Cherawa said as she put out a brown finger to caress the tiny tusk. "Nobody can keep any secrets from him."

"Peekew is gone to speak with the Naga today," Rayang remarked as he hurried on with his drilling and polishing. "Lucky I have a few of those old Punan beads I can fill out with. We will make the front of the necklace of the teeth of the monkey and use the beads for the back. We will put the tusk right in the middle, to give it balance."

"What shall I say when people remark about my new necklace?" Cherawa wanted to know.

"Tell them Chief Rayang has made a gift to his daughter," said her father with dignity; "that will be answer enough."

Cherawa knew that the boar's tusk was one of her father's most valued treasures. It had been passed down to him from the old chief, his father, and bore a reputation for being a carrier of good luck. It had failed in a few notable instances, but was still potent enough to command respect in the village. Peekew had offered a large price for it, having a wish to add it to his collection of charms, but Rayang could never bring himself to part with it.

"Do you think the Naga will say anything to Peekew?" Cherawa questioned. "Do you think Peekew will be without fear when he sees the Naga there on the riverbank?"

"Hush, child; it is not good for us to inquire into the doings of the witch doctor and the Naga. The spirits are powerful. We are fortunate to have Peekew to deal with them and to advise us how we may avoid their displeasure."

"Father, did the men from the white boat worship the spirits?" Cherawa recalled the simple devotions of the three visitors who had spent the previous night in the village.

"Child, you disturb me. Look, I have made the hole in this tooth too low down. Go find your brother and amuse yourself with him." Rayang scowled and examined the monkey tooth with displeasure, although Cherawa could see nothing the matter with it.

So Cherawa left her father at his important work and tripped down the long inner veranda of the long house; past old Nagal the leper, who lay all the time on his sleeping mat; past the clusters of heads fastened to the overhead beams, until she came to her own door. There she met Dawee with a couple of deep baskets in her hands.

"Get your paddle and come with me, Cherawa," her mother commanded. Without a word Cherawa took down her paddle from its place on the wall and followed Dawee down the notched log ladder into their small dugout canoe. This was not the big canoe of Rayang with the carved bird on its prow, but a small boat which Dawee reserved for her own excursions on the river.

Dawee scanned the sandbank close to the village. "Why don't we see your golden crocodile around here any more?" she asked Cherawa.

"I think she has a mate now, and she doesn't come to the village so often. I saw her a few days ago and gave her a ball of rice." Cherawa rowed with practiced skill.

"You must not fail to present her with proper offerings when she comes around," the mother instructed Cherawa. "Remember, the spirit of the stranger lives in her."

"What are we going after?" Cherawa changed the subject.

"We are going to gather leaves for dyeing. We must dye yarn for new skirts for both of us, and our old ones could do with a little freshening." Dawee guided the canoe down the river, keeping close to the bank and looking at the shrubbery as they passed along.

Not far downstream Dawee nosed the dugout into the bank and tied it fast to a tree root. Both of them scrambled out, and Dawee began plucking the leaves from an ordinary-looking bush which grew in abun-

After gathering leaves for dyeing, Dawee and Cherawa rowed upstream.

dance on that spot. Cherawa helped until both baskets were full and pressed down. After loading the baskets in the canoe, they turned the nose of their craft upstream and, with some diligent effort, soon brought it to the home wharf.

"Mother, don't you think Peekew will be back soon? Do you think he will stay long with the Naga?" Cherawa could not forget the witch doctor.

"I am afraid after Peekew sees the Naga, he will come home and lay a ban on the village. Then of course nobody can come into the village or leave it for no one knows how long. That's why I hurried to get these leaves this morning. I must finish this dyeing, so I can get all the weaving done before the rice harvest begins." Dawee looked troubled.

All that afternoon Cherawa tended the large earthen pot in which Dawee boiled the leaves. After the pot started to boil, she threw in the skeins of cotton yarn for weaving, also a couple old skirts that had faded. The pot boiled and boiled. Cherawa brought more and more wood to keep the fire going.

At last Dawee took a long stick and fished out the things she had meant to dye. She laid them dripping in a basket. The color of them had not changed at all. The cotton yarn she had purchased from the Chinese merchant was still white. The skirts were still faded, but Dawee knew her dye.

She picked up the basket, carried it down to the edge of the river, and threw the whole load into the mud, which was soft and black and deep on the right side of the log wharf. Both Dawee and Cherawa began stomping the clothes and the yarn into the mud and working them around in it with their feet. This process continued for half an hour. Then Dawee picked her material out of the mud, carried it onto the wharf, and washed it clean in the clear water of the river. All had turned a dull black color.

"Black as a wild pig," said Cherawa. Dawee hung up her dyed goods with much satisfaction.

Cherawa could hardly wait to return to her father and see what progress had been made with her necklace. Relieved of further responsibility, she scampered back to where the chief still sat on the outer veranda. He was not alone. Mapang was with him. The two were engaged in earnest conversation.

"Look," Mapang spoke in a low voice, but with great agitation; "it was the same day you saw the Naga that these strangers showed up with their plan to build a medicine house and a teaching house across the river from this village."

"It does look like the two have some connection. We must watch these strangers and be constantly on guard, although I must say they seem harmless enough." Rayang was still drilling and polishing.

"Of course we may be able to get a lot of medicine from them, and they may be useful to us in other ways; but we must be careful. I have a feeling that they intend to change the customs on this river." Mapang scratched as he talked. The ringworm on his body made curious whorls and curves. He was covered with it from head to foot, as were all the other inhabitants of Rayang's village.

The three men had left early that morning after expressing their thanks for the night's lodging. They had taken a couple bottles of kerosene out of their boat and left them, together with two measures of sugar and two of salt, as a token of their friendship and esteem. The white launch had gone down the river and had not returned. Perhaps it would never return. Anyhow, Cherawa reasoned, with a powerful charm like the galeega, she need not fear the strangers. No, no, there was no need to be afraid—but Cherawa was afraid!

What did the Naga signify? Was it an evil omen? Perhaps the great sickness was coming again. Perhaps her own father or mother might be stricken. The coming of these strange men might forebode evil. Oh, there was much to fear!

The polishing of the monkey teeth was too long a job to be accomplished in one day. The chief of Rayang intended this piece of work to be a credit to his own craftsmanship, as well as a powerful charm for his daughter. He worked with great care. Then evening came, and purple shadows lengthened around the long house. Since it was too dark to see, Rayang gathered up his materials; and the whole village, each family within its own door, went through the usual bedtime chores and prepared to go to sleep. The people had not enjoyed much sleep in the long house the previous night, for the excitement of the three strange men and their medicine had been too much.

Cherawa found it impossible to settle down to sleep. She heard the heavy breathing of her parents and knew that they slept. Chendang always slept soundly in spite of his ringworm. No one could awaken him except with violence. Cherawa rose from her sleeping mat and crept out the door. She crossed the inner veranda, went past old Nagal the leper, who slept on his mat in the open air, and out to the wide-open porch which had no roof and lay open to the moonlight.

She hung over the railing and watched the flowing river. Something in the sure movement of the water stilled the tumult of apprehension in Cherawa's mind. She waited and watched till the moon climbed to midheaven.

She was thinking of returning to her sleeping mat. Just then a movement on the inner veranda drew her attention. Someone was descending the notched log ladder. It was Treesa! It must be that Treesa has an appointment with the spirits tonight. Cherawa sighed a deep sigh. Treesa's devotion to the spirits was well known and respected, but it was no special benefit to her family. Her husband, Garyu, was often left alone all night with the two babies. After spending so much time with the spirits, she had little time to cook or weave or help with the rice planting and harvesting, so the family was poor and often ill fed. They would have been little regarded among their fellow villagers had it not been for Treesa's close dealings with the spirits. She was held in awe, and her warnings were always respected.

"It seems a pity," Cherawa spoke to herself, "that all the spirits are so much against us. I wonder why they are so cruel. I hate that dreadful Naga! How could such a horrible creature portend anything but evil?"

Now that she had put her fear into words, Cherawa felt worse, but she recalled the galeega and comforted herself. Would the galeega avail even against the powerful medicine of the Naga, against the medicine of the three strangers from the white boat? She made her way back to her sleeping mat, but she slept poorly all night, for the ringworm was troublesome, and she had snatches of dreams. In them the Naga appeared as huge as the river, and it seemed to be bearing her swiftly away. She woke in terror. It was broad daylight and she was alone.

Evening came again before Peekew finally returned. He had visited the Naga and other places, including the piece of ground across the river where the new village was to be built.

The village buzzed with excitement. "Peekew says the Naga is making powerful medicine," Treesa announced to the group of women taking their evening bath near the log wharf. "Soon everyone will know about it."

"Is it good medicine or bad medicine?" Cherawa wanted to be practical.

"He didn't say," Dawee put in. "I suppose it must be bad."

"The ban begins tomorrow," said another woman. "What a shame! Our rice field has been doing so well, but of course the wild pigs and the deer will ruin it if we can't leave the village to watch it."

"None of us can look after our gardens while the ban is on," complained another of the bathers. "What will we eat if the deer and wild pigs and birds eat all our rice?"

"The spirits and their omens must be respected," Treesa said with a stern face. "Better go hungry than offend the spirits."

The women all knew that Treesa was right. How

fortunate they were to have a skilled witch doctor like Peekew who could communicate with the Naga and let them know what to do! What a protection to the village! With heavy hearts they crept back up the notched log in the early darkness.

The men were in conference. It had already been decided that the village should go under the ban on the morrow. No one could leave or enter the village for the duration of this taboo, and it would be lifted only at the word of the witch doctor.

Peekew had explored across the river and reported that there was nothing there except a few stakes made of peeled saplings stuck here and there in the ground. It was his opinion that the strangers would be back. He assured the villagers that the appearance of the Naga on Sungi Sap at the same time as the first arrival of the strangers was an exceedingly bad omen. "The spirits are against them," he said with an ominous shake of his head; "we cannot afford to offend the spirits."

So the village was closed to all traffic. No one came in and no one went out. It was the season when the rice was in the milk, not many weeks before harvest. Every bird and beast in the jungle seemed to have uncanny knowledge of when the rice was heading out. They all gathered to feast on it or to dig it up or foul it in some way. Every person who was at all provident or diligent kept watch day and night over the fields to scare away the marauders and ensure a food supply for the coming year. The fields were not near the village, but were a half hour's rowing up the river. There the forest had been cleared and burned to prepare for the planting. Every year a new place was chosen; and the heavy work of felling the trees, clearing the brush, and burning off the whole thing had to be done all over again.

Despite the ban life went on as usual. Mapang busied himself with making knives. He was the best blacksmith in the village. His knives were always in demand. Garyu worried over his wife's spending so much time with the spirits while he cooked and tended the babies. Chief Rayang worked on the necklace of monkey teeth. Dawee began weaving some new skirts for Cherawa and herself. Peekew mended his fish nets and put his charms in order. All the villagers chewed hard on their quids of betel nut and thought constantly of the lush fields of rice now being ravaged by the wild creatures of the forest.

In the last room of the long house Garyu's father lay sick with a fever. Peekew visited him at intervals and applied his charms, but the future did not look good. Peekew noted that the old man had no possessions beyond a few simple things—his mat, a pot or two, and baskets and nets. It was not a profitable case, and as the days went by, Peekew's indifference lapsed into open neglect.

CHAPTER FOUR

UNDER THE BAN

AT LAST the necklace was finished. "There, Little One," said the chief as he fastened it around his daughter's neck; "you have the finest necklace on the river." Then he bent to whisper in her ear, "Also the most powerful charm."

"Father," Cherawa looked up into her father's smiling face, "may I use the charm on Garyu's father? It might cure him of his fever."

"Certainly, child, that is very thoughtful of you. Peekew isn't doing anything for the old man."

Cherawa slipped away and crept in the door of the last room in the village. The sick man lay on his mat in the corner. His face was flushed with fever, and his breathing was rapid. His bloodshot eyes followed Cherawa as she came into the room. He muttered something about "white round things." He seemed to be in a delirium. Cherawa came close to him. She had slipped

Cherawa's necklace, made by her father, was the finest on the river.

the necklace into her hand. She laid the small tusk against his arm.

"Child," said the sick man in a weak voice, "when the strangers were here several nights ago, the smiling one gave me some small, white round things. He said they were powerful medicine."

The old man fumbled with his mat. "Where are the small, white round things?" Cherawa asked. He tapped on his sleeping mat with a bony finger. Cherawa lifted the corner of the mat and drew out a small piece of banana leaf. Four tiny white things were folded in it. To the amazement of Cherawa, the sick man took the leaf in his hand and swallowed them all.

When morning came, Cherawa was the first one awake. She looked in the door at the sick man. He was sitting on his mat chewing a fat quid of betel nut. Her heart did a quick flip-flop. The galeega had scored one! Then she went on her way to pound rice on the veranda of the long house.

"Where did you get your necklace?" It was Cherawa's friend Jeria who put the question.

"My father made it for a present for me." Cherawa fondled the tiny boar's tusk that hung as a pendant from her throat.

"It is beautiful!" Jeria's admiration was genuine. She had a few small trinkets of her own, but none to compare with the new necklace that Cherawa had worn around her neck with such pride for several days.

"The tusk is an old charm that belonged to my grandfather," Cherawa confided; "it is strong medicine. Only last night I took it to Garyu's father and laid it against his arm. This morning he was well from his fever."

"Yes, he did seem to feel better this morning, but I understand he is worse again this afternoon. The fever has come back, and he doesn't know anyone, not even his own son." Jeria lifted the heavy rice pounder and went to work with vigor.

A chill clutched at the heart of Cherawa. Was the galeega then of no value? What had she failed to do? She thought of the four tiny white things that the old man had swallowed. She should have prevented him, for they were the white man's medicine. True, they all had sampled the white man's medicine that night when the strangers slept in their village, but this was different, secretlike and mysterious. How terrible! She could not tell anyone about it! Everyone would blame her for allowing the old man to swallow the foreign medicine. Now he would probably die. Cherawa lifted her rice pounder and began the even up-and-down strokes that separated the shucks from the good rice.

For several days no sign of life had appeared across the river. It had been watched by dozens of keen eyes. The white launch had gone down the river, and it had not come back. In spite of this, the talk of the whole village was about the strangers and their intentions.

Late the next afternoon a noise of distant throbbing was heard on the river. Everyone crowded to the outer veranda platform. The sound came nearer. All the villagers drew in deep breaths as a large launch rounded the curve of the river below the village. It was not the white launch, but a much larger boat.

"It is the 'Motor Chin,' " Mapang informed everyone. The "Motor Chin" was a freight launch belonging to a Chinese merchant. On rare occasions it had been seen before, but never so far up the river as this. Every eye was fastened on the approaching boat. It lay low in the water as though hauling a heavy load. The suspense was almost more than anyone could bear.

The launch pulled in close to the one floating log on the opposite shore of the river. It was made fast, and the sound of its throbbing motor ceased. Several people scrambled out and began unloading the launch. It was too far away to see what was being unloaded, although every eye in Rayang Village was strained to the utmost. The dusk was falling, and the curiosity of every watcher became almost painful.

Now under ordinary circumstances half a dozen boats would have put off at first sight of the launch. They would have crossed over and found out at close range just what was going on. But a ban was on the village. The fear of the Naga was terrible. His curses, if he chose to distribute any, would certainly fall on the village of Chief Rayang, for it was nearest. Peekew had done the best he could for the protection of everyone. Also, he had made sure that if the appearance of the Naga should by any faint chance portend good, no other village would share in it. He had spread the word up and down the river that no one was to go up Sungi Sap because the Naga was busy with great contemplations and did not wish to be disturbed further. Cherawa knew all this, but still she wanted to climb into her dugout and paddle across the river more than she had wanted to do anything else in all her life.

Then another sound broke the stillness of the evening. The white launch was arriving. It was made fast to the large boat, as the single log that served for a wharf was not big enough to accommodate both launches.

Deep sighs were heard among the group watching from the veranda of Rayang's village. Peekew coughed several times. The night fell, and the villagers sought their own quarters. That is, most of them did. Peekew and Mapang lingered in the outer porch, chewing hard on their betel nut and thinking about what these new developments might signify.

Cherawa also could not tear herself away. A bright light on the large launch threw a beam on the landing place near it. She supposed the unloading of the launch was still going on. Chief Rayang went into his room and came out several times.

An hour passed. Then a faint sound of oars was heard on the river. A voice hailed the dark figures leaning over the rail of the outer veranda. "Friends, brothers!" it called in pleasant tones. "Deckie calling you. I have medicine for the sick man in your village. He has fever. I gave him medicine when we were here last week, but he must have more if he is to get well." A short silence ensued. "Come, friends, come down to the wharf and get the medicine."

Peekew cleared his throat; then his deep, mellow voice rang out over the water: "This village is under a ban. None of us can go out or come in. No medicine can go out or come in. Please go away and do not disturb us."

Late that night, or perhaps it was even early morning, Cherawa sat up on her mat startled out of her sleep. She listened. A steady sound of "tunk-tunk-tunk" came from the darkness. It sounded like a stone being dropped into a deep hole with a plunking sound. It was repeated again in less than a minute. Cherawa clutched her heart in terror. It was the voice of the omen bird. It was near. It sounded as though he must be perched right on the roof of the long house. Only once before in her life had she heard the voice of the omen bird. Only once before had it perched on the roof of their village. A few days later Garyu's mother had died.

It was still very dark, but other noises cut their way into her senses. A terrible creaking noise began, together with a squealing and the voice of chanting.

Cherawa was afraid to go out. She was afraid of what she would find when she opened the door. Her parents were not on their sleeping mats. They must be outside. Then the fear of the unknown rose strong within her and compelled her to creep out of the door.

A dim light was burning before the last door in the village. A spirit swing had been set up before the door —a well-polished length of hardwood log hung from the overhead beams with heavy cords of rattan. Every time the swing moved back and forth, it creaked with a loud and terrible noise. Indai Mapang and Indai Jeria ("Indai Mapang" means "Mother of Mapang") were sitting in the spirit swing, swaying slowly back and forth. At their feet lay a pig, tied in such an uncomfortable position that it squealed continuously. The two women added to the nerve-racking sounds a chant of such dolefulness that Cherawa shuddered, although she had heard it often enough before to know that it was the usual chant for the dying.

"The old man must be going," Cherawa conjectured. "How dreadful! How dreadful!" She lingered in the shadows, and she was not alone. Many of the villagers had been disturbed in their rest and had come out into the dark veranda. Cherawa felt a warm hand laid on her shoulder. It was her father, Rayang the chief.

With her hand clutching her father's, Cherawa walked to the door of the last room in the village and looked in. Garyu's father lay on his mat. His son and daughter-in-law knelt beside him. His breath was coming hard and fast. His face was flushed with fever. He appeared to have no consciousness of what was going on.

In the dim light from a wick of cotton in a coconut oil lamp Peekew could be seen. He was sitting cross-legged beside the sick man, with several of his charms spread before him. Among them was a cluster of seeds. The seeds were black and highly polished. They glistened a little in the faint light. There were perhaps a dozen of them. Each seed had a tiny hole bored in the end, and a small thong of skin was attached to each. The whole cluster was tied together with a knot. Peekew tossed this charm into the air and let it fall. He counted the seeds that fell toward the sick man, and the seeds that fell away from him. Of the whole cluster only three seeds fell toward the father of Garyu. The rest of the seeds fell away on the far side.

Peekew shook his head, gathered up his charms,

and began a chant in his deep, musical voice. But it could scarcely be heard for the squealing of the pig, the creaking of the spirit swing, and the chanting of the two women.

So the morning broke. It was now almost two weeks since the ban had been laid on Rayang's village. The horrid noises that sped the dying man on his journey to the spirit world never ceased all that day and continued on into the following night. Then the chants gave way to violent shrieks of weeping and wailing as Indai Mapang took up her appointed task as chief mourner.

The death of Garyu's father necessitated the lifting of the ban, for the body must be taken to the burial tree up the river. It would be well wrapped in bark and securely tied in the branches of the chosen tree. The spirit of the departed would be lulled to quietness by the music of the ever-flowing stream. It was hoped by all that the spirit would find sufficient contentment to prevent its ever returning to annoy any of the villagers.

On the way home from the burial, some of the villagers went to have a look at their neglected rice fields. Cherawa stood among the tall stalks of rice in her father's garden. There was not much left. The deer had cropped it on all sides. The wild pigs had rooted in the best of it, and the birds had shelled out many of the fat kernels. What remained was not yet ready to gather. There was so little of it left. It seemed of no use to give it any attention.

Everyone headed for the tuan's new project with a feeling that troubles could be forgotten for the moment, while they made an investigation of what they had been dying to know about for days.

Several boats were tied up at the one log that served as a landing place. No launch was visible. A great many boards and heavy timbers were arranged in drying racks, curing for use in future building. There was nothing else to see, so the visitors from Rayang untied their boats and paddled home.

"My Father," began Cherawa as she sat in the dugout with the chief and plied a skillful paddle, "why didn't my galeega work on Garyu's father? Was it because he took the white tuan's medicine?"

There was no longer any secret about the medicine, for Deckie had shouted in the ears of the whole village that he had left medicine for the sick man.

"It is probably not good to mix the spirit medicine and the tuan's medicine," Rayang replied after some thought. "We should not lose faith in the galeega. It is the most powerful of charms. There is no question about that!"

Thus comforted, Cherawa said no more. When they tied the dugout at the home wharf, she scurried up the notched log with a lightness she had not felt for days.

It was the following morning when Cherawa saw the tawny golden crocodile on the sand bar at the left side of the log wharf. As far as the village folk could tell, the crocodile had come to their village at the time Cherawa was born, to be her special guardian. Since she was a different color from all the other crocodiles in the river, it was always easy to recognize Cherawa's strange pet; and the ugly creature was held in much respect by Rayang's village.

Cherawa hurried to find a ball of rice for the "Golden Lady," as she called her.

Coming down to the wharf, Cherawa laid the ball of rice on the very edge of the log nearest the crocodile; then she folded her arms and waited.

The crocodile crawled very slowly with clumsy movements of her great claws. She lifted her head and swallowed the ball of rice. Cherawa danced with delight, as she always did when the Golden Lady accepted her small offerings of food.

Then Cherawa stepped very lightly toward the crocodile. The animal did not move. Another long step and Cherawa was near enough to touch the crocodile's horny head. She pulled off her necklace and rubbed the shiny little boar's tusk along the horny plates of the animal's head. "Ah, my pretty one, my

Golden Lady, this is the greatest charm known on this river. It will make you a good crocodile." So saying, she slipped the necklace back over her head with a merry laugh, and the tawny beast slid back into the river.

"There, now," she said to herself, "my charm is even stronger; the strength of the Golden Lady has gone into it."

Cherawa knew that none of the rest of the villagers dared to approach any crocodile. It would enhance the value of her charm to have dedicated it in a certain sense to the crocodile. Cherawa also had a secret hope that the cream-colored crocodile would maintain her good behavior. The charm might make sure of that.

CHAPTER FIVE

A SONG IN THE RIVER

"MY WIFE is ailing," Garyu complained to Chief Rayang; "she has not been well for days, and now that my father is dead, she feels worse."

"What seems to be wrong with her?" the chief inquired with kindness.

"The spirits told her a moon ago that she should eat no more fruit. She stopped eating fruit. Then three days ago the spirits told her she must eat no more rice." Garyu looked worried. He held his smallest baby boy in his arms. The tiny fellow looked thin and wailed pitifully all the while Garyu was talking. "I think the baby is hungry." Garyu looked lovingly down at the little one and rocked it back and forth in his arms to quiet its wailing.

"See what Peekew can do about it," suggested the chief, looking with sympathy on the young father and

Cherawa willingly helped soothe the cries of Treesa's two babies.

the hungry crying baby. Garyu walked off in search of the witch doctor.

"Father, why would the spirits tell Treesa not to eat?" Cherawa looked worried. "Don't the spirits know that her little baby will have no milk if she eats nothing?"

"Yes, of course the spirits know all that." Rayang scratched his head. "But the spirits are cruel. They have no pity for the sufferings of little children. The thing to do is to find out what is causing their displeasure; then maybe they will let Treesa eat again."

"But Treesa is devoted to the spirits. She is always meeting them in secret places in the jungle and trying to find out what the spirits think and plan. It looks like they would be more kind to her." Cherawa felt that it was all very unfair.

"Hush, child; it is not good to question the doings of the spirits." Rayang scowled. "It might make them angry with us. We must find something that Treesa can eat. Perhaps she could eat some fish. It looks like a good night for fishing. Will you help Treesa mind the two babies while Garyu goes fishing with me?"

Cherawa hastened to consent and took up her wearying task of soothing the cries of both little fellows. Treesa lay on her mat. Her eyes held that faraway look that Cherawa knew so well. She looked thin and tired, but she was talkative.

"I have always tried to do everything the spirits told me to do," the young mother began. "Many times I have felt the spirits shiver my body with their power. They are very strong. They could easily tear one in pieces."

Cherawa shuddered but said nothing. She was thinking some hard thoughts about the spirits, but dared not express them for fear some of Treesa's familiar spirits might be lurking in the room. She turned the conversation to the developments across the river. The two chattered for a couple of hours about the tuan and his medicine and the man Jesus, in whose name the strangers said they had come.

"I suppose this Jesus is a high government official," said Treesa. "He must be fairly well off to have sent all that lumber up for building."

"That little teacher, Deckie, pointed straight up in the sky. He said Jesus lives up there," Cherawa recalled.

"Of course no one but spirits could live up in the air," Treesa remarked; "I'm sure Jesus is no spirit. They said Jesus told them to bring medicine, too. No, I'm sure Jesus must be a high officer. Perhaps He will show up around here one of these days, and we will get a look at Him."

Under the faithful supervision of Cherawa both babies slept at last. It was late when Garyu returned. He had a nice catch of fish and had already cooked them over the fire in Rayang's kitchen. Treesa sat up on her mat with a wan smile. Garyu bent over her with tender care, smoothing back her dark hair and coaxing her to eat. Cherawa slipped out of the room and went to her sleeping mat.

"Cherawa, Cherawa, wake up, wake up!" It was Chendang shaking her awake in the early morning. "The white launch is coming up the river. Let's go and see it!"

Cherawa always wore the same clothes night and day. All the people in the village did so. There was little ceremony to arising in the morning, but an early bath was important. The two children raced down the notched log to the water, leaped in, and came up blowing and sputtering. From the water they clambered into the smallest dugout and made off across the river without telling anyone where they went. Since the Iban parents exercise little supervision over their children, this was no unusual thing. Also Chendang was a little afraid he might be forbidden the trip to the new village if he mentioned it.

The white launch was already tied alongside the landing when they arrived. The dugout was made fast, and they scrambled out.

"We have early visitors," remarked Deckie with his usual smile. "So the ban has been lifted?" He raised his eyebrows as he questioned Chendang. "Tell me," he inquired with interest, "how is the man who was sick with fever?"

"He is dead," Chendang answered with a grave face.

A look of sharp sadness crossed the face of Deckie. "I'm so sorry!"

Cherawa and Chendang left Deckie and sat on their heels in the shade of a great tree near the landing and observed many things. "Look, Cherawa, they have a Chinese boat." Chendang pointed to a well-built rowboat larger than the usual dugout canoe and painted white like the launch.

"And they have a dugout, too," Cherawa remarked, eyeing a new canoe, also tied at the landing.

Two Chinese men were marking out a large square just back of the landing. It appeared likely that there was going to be a building there. Timbers were being placed, and the work was about to begin.

Deckie and the tuan were busy, too. They helped with the measuring and the selection of timbers. Often they stopped work to look on a large sheet of paper with some marks on it.

Cherawa and Chendang were not the only watchers. A boatload of men from the village of Sidang came ashore and stood or squatted watching with eager faces. From Sawa's village down the river came crippled Jurumpoo and his shriveled little mother, wife of Chief Sawa. Jurumpoo sat in the boat, but his mother came ashore to see what was going on.

From Biban and Sap and Tatau Fort representatives were also present. They squatted near the landing place, chewed on their quids of betel nut, and looked and chatted.

"I can't see why that white man wants to come here and live in the Iban country. He doesn't know the customs. The spirits will not favor him. It looks like he would stay among his own people." The wife of Sawa thus expressed her opinion.

"They say a man called Jesus told them to come here and bring us medicine and good news," a man from Sidang said.

"What good news can they bring us? Can they bring us news that the government won't collect taxes any more? Can they bring us news that we won't have to work so hard clearing jungle? Can they bring us news that the wild pigs will let our rice alone?" The wife of Sawa spat on the ground. "Bah!" she said; "I'll listen to their good news when they can cure the rheumatism in my back!"

Everyone laughed loudly at this, for the aches and pains of this good lady were known up and down the river. The witch doctors had tried all their charms on her, but in vain.

A young man from Sidang Village named Nuri,

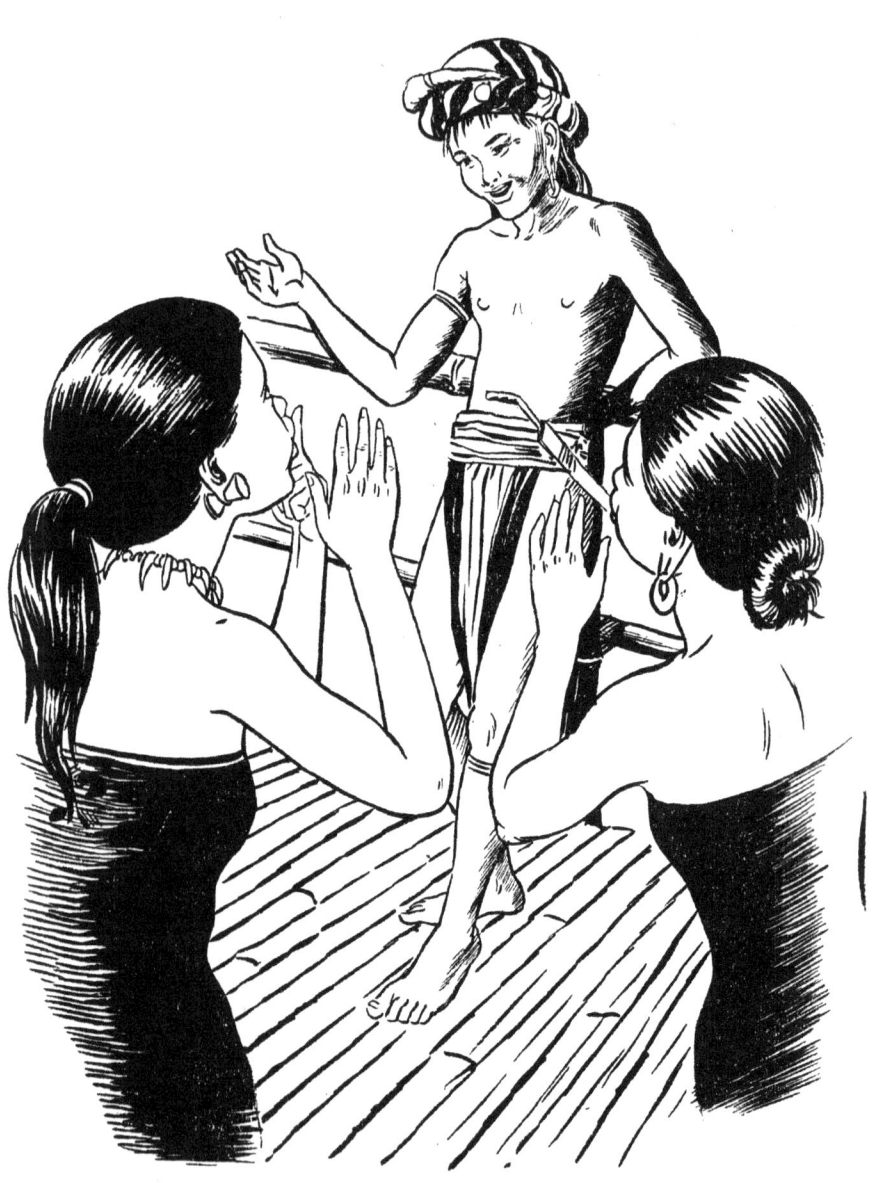

Nuri, a fine young man from another village, spoke highly of Deckie.

with a broad smile on his handsome face, spoke next: "I have talked some with Deckie. He says this man Jesus is the Son of Tuan Allah, the great Creator who lives in the heavens. And there is with them a great and good Spirit who is everywhere and loves everyone. He says that these three made the river, the forest, the rice, the sky, all the animals—everything!" Nuri spread his hands wide to include them all. "Deckie is a fine fellow!"

Several of the men shifted their position. They scowled and seemed to be displeased that so young a man had spoken.

The wife of Sawa was already leaving, but she flung one parting remark over her shoulder. "What nonsense! If Jesus is the Son of the Great Spirit, then He must be a spirit, too. How then can He be a man?" With that she flounced into her boat and pulled away. All the men sitting on their heels laughed again. They nodded to one another and spat betel nut juice far and near, but the look on their faces seemed to indicate that they thought the old lady was pretty cute, and they agreed more or less with what she had said. Nuri, however, was troubled, and he went to stand beside Deckie. Cherawa and Chendang followed him. Cherawa was sure that Nuri was going to ask Deckie more about the man Jesus.

"Teacher Deckie," Nuri began in a low voice, "if

Jesus is the Son of the Great Spirit that made all things, how then can He be a man? Men are not spirits."

Deckie smiled his beautiful smile. "Come," he said, "let us sit here and I will tell you the story."

The four of them sat on their heels near the new building site. The group near the wharf figured that Nuri had asked Deckie a hard question, and now they came straggling up, one by one. All of them squatted in a circle about Deckie.

"The Great Spirit, Tuan Allah, made all things," Deckie began. "He made the light; He made the sun, the moon, and the stars. He made the plants, flowers, trees, vines, the rice, and the grass. He made them all. He made all the animals. He made the river and the ocean. Last of all He made a man and a woman, and all the other things He made were for them. He loved everything He had made. It was beautiful and good. Most of all He loved the man and woman. But an evil spirit was at work, too. This evil spirit hated Tuan Allah. He corrupted many of the good spirits who were Tuan Allah's helpers, and made them into demons. It is these demons of which you are all so much afraid." Deckie paused. The listeners exchanged knowing glances, but said nothing.

"This prince of evil spirits set about to destroy all that Tuan Allah had made. He hated Tuan Allah so much that he spent all his time trying to ruin the beautiful world. Tuan Allah was patient for many years. Finally when men had become very wicked, He sent His only Son Jesus into the world as a tiny baby, born of a woman of this earth. Tuan Allah wanted His Son, Jesus, to live among men to show them how much Tuan Allah loves them. He stayed here in this world for over thirty years. Then wicked men killed Him."

The group around Deckie had been listening with their full attention. Now excited whispers arose. "If He was killed, then how could He send you here?" The question was on everybody's lips.

Deckie paused and smiled to them all. "You see, the Father of Jesus, the great Tuan Allah, is the center of all life and power. Jesus also had the power to live again within Himself, just like a seed has power to grow up out of the ground after it is dead and buried. After three days Jesus rose up from the dead and went back to live with His Father in heaven. Yet He is still a man. He will always be so. He loves all men, and especially He loves the little children because He was Himself once an earthly child."

Cherawa clutched at her charm. What kind of teaching was this? If these words were true, then Jesus was not at all like the familiar jungle spirits. "He loves little children." The rest of what Deckie had said Cherawa dimly comprehended without believing it at all. Each village had storytellers. They could all tell tall yarns. Deckie was evidently the storyteller for this new village of the tuan. But this Jesus must be somebody real; anyhow, He was real enough so this whole new project was going forward at His command. And "He loves little children." The words sang themselves over and over again into the heart of Cherawa. Jesus would not tell Treesa to go without food and starve her poor baby! No, no, not if He loves little children!

Cherawa and Chendang returned to their dugout and paddled home without any talk between them.

Jeria and Cherawa were at their usual task of pounding out rice early the next morning after the visit to Bukit Nyala, as the tuan's village was now called. The word "Bukit" means "a hill," and "Nyala" means "the shining of a light." So the name meant "The Hill of the Shining Light," a pretty name indeed. But there was still nothing on the hill. There was only the beginning of a house at the landing.

"Do you know that Teacher Deckie and his wife are going to stay at the long house of Sidang?" Jeria paused in her hard work. "He has a wife and a baby girl, too. They will live at Sidang until their house is ready over there by the river."

"Oh, why didn't they come here!" exclaimed Cherawa. "It is so much closer!" Cherawa spoke out of the real feeling in her heart. She liked Deckie; his smile was beautiful to see. He was kind and a wonderful storyteller. What fun it would be to sit around in the evenings and listen to Deckie's stories! "Well, I guess they might have come here, but this village was under the ban. And Mapang and Peekew are not very friendly to the strangers. I think your father, the chief, was afraid to have them come."

Cherawa remembered the words of Nuri, the youth from Sidang Village. She recalled how friendly he had seemed to the young teacher. She knew that Deckie had found one true friend among the Ibans.

That evening after the sun had gone down and the moon had risen above Mount Biban, the villagers sat in the veranda of the long house and discussed the events of the past few weeks. Suddenly Peekew left his place in the circle and stepped into the outer porch. A faint sound was heard on the river. Everyone crowded to the railing overlooking the river. There was a sound of singing, sweet and clear. It drifted through the night like a wave of peace. It was in the Iban language. Everyone could understand the words of the beautiful song.

> "Everybody ought to love Jesus, Jesus, Jesus.
> He died on the cross to save us from sin;
> Everybody ought to love Jesus."

Over and over the words were repeated, until the

sweet melody hung but faintly in the air and the words faded in the distance.

The boat had passed on up the river. No one doubted that the singer was Deckie, but part of the time there were two voices. It sounded as though Deckie might be trying to teach the song to someone. "Nuri! Nuri!" thought Cherawa to herself. She figured it must be that after the day's work was done, Nuri and the new teacher were paddling home to Sidang, and Nuri was learning the song "Everybody Ought to Love Jesus." Well, she would learn it, too. It was not hard to learn. She hummed the tune over to herself as she went to bed. During the night she wakened often, and always the tune came back like a light in her heart. She could remember every word of the song as she sang softly to herself.

The Ibans sang songs, too, but they were different. They made them up as they went along, and never sang the same song twice. Their songs were weird chants. Cherawa had heard one that day. There was a traveler passing along the river, and his song ran thus:

> "I see that the white man is building a house,
> The white man is building a house.
> I see that his white boat is tied to a log,
> His boat is tied to a log.
> The white man wants to bring medicine.
> The white man wants to bring new customs,
> But the Iban doesn't want the white man's ways."

CHAPTER SIX

THE EATER OF SOULS

I<small>T WAS</small> at night when the terrible thing happened. All was dark in the village when a swishing sound was heard. A stark terror took possession of everyone in the long house. They cried out in anguish. It was the awful sound that betokened the presence of evil spirits. Everyone ran together. They clutched one another with cold hands and cried out in an agony of fear.

Cherawa felt the awful presence and screamed with the rest. Then her father's hand was laid on her shoulder. He loosened the necklace from her throat and held it high, so everyone could see it by the light of old Nagal's candle.

"Look, all of you!" he shouted above the din. "There is a powerful charm in this necklace. It is a galeega. Please be quiet. The evil spirits will not harm you when so powerful a charm rests in this village."

The people became calm again. The screaming ceased, and order was at last restored. Cherawa realized that her father had been obliged to divulge the secret of the galeega in this time of awful crisis. Nothing else would have sufficed to reassure the villagers.

Peekew came and took the necklace from the hand of the chief. He looked it over with care. Then he tapped on the little polished tusk and looked questioningly into the face of Rayang. The chief nodded as he fastened the necklace again around the neck of his daughter. Sometime after midnight the village sank into a troubled slumber.

"It is Treesa." The troubled face of Garyu appeared at the door of Chief Rayang the next morning. "It is Treesa. The spirits are angry with her because she has been eating fish. They say that from now on she can eat nothing." The young man groaned and turned back to his own room.

Rayang shrugged his shoulders. After all, what could one do? The spirits had made sufficient demonstration to show that they were much displeased about something. It was a relief to know that it was only one person and not the whole village that had fallen under the displeasure of the higher powers.

Cherawa searched her father's face and followed his thoughts in the matter exactly, but her tender heart ached for the little baby of Treesa. It would surely die now. Such a nice little boy, just learning to coo and smile.

"He loves little children; He loves little children." Over and over the words came back to Cherawa. The song "Everybody Ought to Love Jesus" also came to her mind.

Cherawa fondled her charm and thought of the marvelous effect it had on the village the night before. O blessed charm! But then she remembered the words of the song. She ran wildly down to the wharf, the tumult of her thoughts almost more than she could bear.

It had become the custom for most of the people from Rayang Village, as well as for most of the people in the other river villages, to go every day to Bukit Nyala to see how things were progressing there. The river seethed with excitement, and the talk about the doings of the strangers filled the land. No one person could possibly keep up with all the news, though Mapang tried his best to do so. He was everywhere and in everything.

Mapang sold several of his best knives to the strangers, then regretted doing so, and went to a great deal of trouble to lay a curse on every single knife so it would be sure to get broken or cut the user or do damage of some kind. He received salt and kerosene and sugar and black cloth for his knives and felt himself quite rich, and justly so, since he had soundly cursed the knives.

Cherawa stood one day looking at Deckie. What was it that made him so different from the river people? Deckie's wife had come to the river now, and she looked different. So did Nancy, the baby girl. They all looked different. With sudden surprise she realized what the difference was. Their skins were smooth, smooth as the young banana leaf. How could one account for that?

Rasee, the wife of Deckie, was just a girl, tall and glowing like a candle. She and the baby stayed most of the time at the village of Sidang. Nancy was never naked like the village babies. She wore bright little garments, sometimes several different ones in a day. The Sidang people told it abroad that Rasee had a boxful of garments for herself and the baby. She washed clothes in the river every day. She used a thick bar of brown soap and washed all the things very clean. She had a special line to hang them on.

Rasee could sing like a bird. She could sew anything. She had already made a fine mosquito curtain for the chief of Sidang, the only one in the village. She used soap to wash herself and the baby every day. They were a clean family. The villagers had never seen such cleanness.

All the doings of Deckie and his family were reported. Everything they did was of great importance. Peek holes appeared in the walls on both sides of their room, which was in the middle of the village, and a close watch was kept.

It was known that every night and every morning they kneeled beside a black book, and they talked tenderly and intimately with the Jesus who had sent them to Tatau River. Also they sang songs and looked long at the book they were singing from. Their faces were always happy, and they were kind to everyone.

Cherawa never tired of hearing the news from Sidang and only regretted that Deckie and Rasee had not been allowed to come to Rayang's long house.

The rice harvest was now past. The village of Rayang had gathered in its scanty crop—that which the deer, the birds, and the wild pigs had left. It was little enough, and the chief with his principal counselors knew that the village would be suffering famine in a few weeks. The villagers were advised to go out and make gardens, planting sweet potatoes, tapioca, cucumbers, and other vegetables. Most of these things would not mature before the famine began to pinch, but it was well to have the people busy. It took their minds off their troubles and kept them from running so much to Bukit Nyala.

So it came about that the families of the village were somewhat scattered for a time. Some of them

Cherawa talked about Jeria's father's illness as they pounded rice.

even slept at their gardens, although this required considerable courage. What could one family do against the evil spirits?

"My mother is very worried," remarked Jeria to Cherawa one fine morning as the girls worked at their usual task of pounding out rice.

"Your father and mother are sleeping out in their garden, aren't they?" Cherawa rested from her work a moment to gossip with her little friend. Jeria was two years younger than Cherawa, but large for her age and strong. "What is worrying your mother? Is she afraid to stay in the garden?"

"It is my father who is worrying her," Jeria confided. "In the night when it is dark, he goes outside the cabin. Sometimes he is gone for a long time. When he comes back, he always looks pale and says nothing. My mother thinks he has some secret dealing with the evil spirits. Why else would he want to go outside and stay so long?" Jeria was on the verge of tears, but she went on bravely: "Night before last there was some blood around his mouth when he came in. So my mother thinks he is eating the souls of people. You know that man over in Sawa's village died that very day. My mother thinks that father ate the soul of the man, so he had to die."

The awful significance of what Jeria had just said penetrated Cherawa's mind. If this were true, and there was no reason to doubt it, then none of them were safe. If an eater of souls had appeared among them, no one could foretell whose soul would be devoured next. Just anyone might die. It was a terrifying thought.

"My mother is so ashamed," Jeria added. "I think she will not stay at the garden much longer. She is very close to the spirits herself. She would not want to displease them."

At this moment Chendang came up with his new knife. It was one of Mapang's finest. It was as long as a man's arm between the wrist and the shoulder. It was curved a little, and the sharp edge was on the outer curved edge of the knife. The point was slender and very sharp. Both girls examined the knife with interest. It was good to forget the eater of souls for a moment.

"Oh, that is a fine knife." Cherawa felt the keen blade. "Now you will have to work hard clearing jungle." Both girls laughed as Chendang tried to fasten the knife in his belt after the manner of the older men, but it was too long.

"Why don't you sell the knife to the tuan?" Jeria had a bright idea. "He would give you a lot of salt for so good a knife as that. Then we could have salt to eat."

"No, no." Chendang turned away in displeasure.

"The knife is mine. Mapang made it for me, and I will keep it. Go and trade some of your rice for salt if you are so hungry for it."

The girls, still laughing, watched Chendang make his way down the notched log toward the wharf. They saw him enter the boat with his father. They were certainly off on some sort of expedition. Mapang was with them. They pulled away upriver against the swift current.

The gloom imposed on their minds by thoughts of the eater of souls came back, now that the diversion of Chendang's knife was over. There was so much to be sad about, so many worrying things. Cherawa reflected that Treesa was in great trouble. It was now many days since the spirits had forbidden her to eat anything at all. She lay on her mat most of the time. The little baby had cried for days from hunger, but now he, too, lay quite still. Only by his breathing could one tell that life remained in the wasted little body. Jeria and Cherawa looked in at the door often to see whether Treesa might want a drink. She often did. For some reason the spirits had neglected to forbid her to drink water.

There were not many persons in the village these days. Everyone was hunting food, since the rice was nearly gone. Old Nagal, the leper, still lay on his mat in the inner veranda. The clusters of heads, taken in raids on the Punan country, hung from the ceiling. A good-sized bunch hung in front of the door of Rayang. They were hung high on a rafter and were well smoked, since Dawee and Cherawa frequently made a fire under them so they might smell the smoke and be warm and satisfied.

Still, the village had no pleasant aspect for the two girls this fine bright day. They descended the notched log, unloosed the small dugout, and started across the river toward the tuan's new village at Bukit Nyala.

"Look, Cherawa, the medicine house is nearly finished." Jeria pointed with her paddle and thereby lost several yards in the swift current. "And, see, the house by the river is all done."

Both girls clambered ashore with enthusiasm. The wharf was bigger now. Two more logs had been added. One was a huge one, rather flattened as though nature had especially designed it for use in a log wharf.

They skipped past the river house, which was already familiar to them, and approached the medicine house. It was a small frame building perched on the first shelf of the high hill rising above the river. Deckie was on the porch of the building. The tuan was working inside at a wooden shelf. The Chinese were finishing the roof. It was, in fact, almost done.

"Have you come for medicine?" Deckie smiled his engaging smile and beckoned the two girls to come up on the little railed-in porch which was to serve as waiting room for the patients who sought help at this medicine house.

"Is there medicine here already?" Cherawa asked as she looked around to see if any evidences of medicine were visible.

"Not yet," smiled Deckie, "but I have something pretty to show you." He unrolled a sheet of paper, a very large, heavy sheet. On it was a colored picture. It was the first picture on paper that the girls had ever seen. True, they had often seen pictures in the water, when the reflection made a clear scene; but this was no reflection. The girls examined it on both sides and then looked at it with rapt attention.

"See, this man sitting in the middle is Jesus." Deckie pointed to the face of a man dressed in a long, white garment.

"Who are the children?" Jeria pointed to first one and then another of the group surrounding the Man in the white robe.

"Those are the children that He loves. When He was here in this world, the little children followed Him everywhere, and He took time to talk to them; and when He was resting, they often crowded into His arms as you see them here."

"How strong is Jesus?" Cherawa asked as she fingered her charm.

85

Deckie looked into her face for a moment before he spoke. "Jesus is stronger than any man," he replied.

"Is He stronger than the spirits?" Cherawa asked the question with such earnestness that Deckie smiled again as he answered, "Jesus is stronger than all the spirits."

Cherawa still held the tiny polished boar's tusk caressingly between her fingers. She asked no more questions. Perhaps Jesus was even stronger than the galeega. What could she do about that? No, of course that could not be. The galeega was the most powerful charm known to man, and even Jesus could not be stronger than the galeega.

"I wish Jesus would do something about Treesa." Cherawa finally blurted it out.

"What is wrong with Treesa?" Deckie asked in surprise.

"The spirits won't let Treesa eat, and now her baby is going to die. I think she will die, too." Cherawa was in tears.

"Come, girls," said Deckie as he took his paddle in his hand, "I will go with you to see Treesa." The three of them descended to the log wharf. Nuri was just making fast his dugout. "Come, Nuri," Deckie called him, "come with me."

Without a word Nuri motioned Deckie to enter his boat, and the two canoes skimmed across the river in the direction of Rayang's village. Deckie had not been back to the village since the night he had come offering medicine for Garyu's father. Now he made Nuri's boat fast to the wharf of Rayang and followed the two girls up into the village and into the door where Garyu and Treesa lived.

"Jesus has sent me to help you," Deckie announced to Garyu, who was sitting beside his wife's mat holding the smallest baby in his arms.

Garyu raised his eyes to Deckie's face, but there was no light in them. His face was set in lines of perpetual sadness. He looked down again at the faintly gasping child in his arms.

Deckie knelt beside the little family. "Oh, my friends, Jesus will help you if you will let Him. He is stronger than all men. He is stronger than the spirits. If Jesus tells Treesa to eat, the spirits cannot hurt her."

"Young man," Treesa said as she raised up on her elbow, "all my life I have obeyed the spirits. What kind of talk is this against the spirits? Who is this Jesus you talk about? I do not know Him." Exhausted by this effort, she sank back on her mat and breathed fast and hard. She closed her eyes and lay still.

"Have the spirits forbidden the baby to eat?" Deckie wanted to know. Garyu did not raise his eyes again, but shook his head to show that of course the spirits did not need to tell the baby not to eat. If there was no milk in his mother's breasts, what was the baby to do? It was such a tiny baby.

Deckie motioned to Nuri, and the two left. They hurried down the ladder and into Nuri's boat. They paddled away across the river toward Bukit Nyala. Cherawa and Jeria watched them go with heavy hearts.

"It's too bad Treesa won't let them help her." Cherawa spoke with tears in her voice.

"It is too late," cried Jeria; "the Jesus teaching has come too late!"

"Do you remember," asked Cherawa, "the time when the crocodile overturned the boat of Garyu and grabbed Treesa by the shoulder? Do you remember how Garyu fought the crocodile until he let her go, and do you remember how he watched over her day and night until she began to get well again?"

Both girls were thinking the same thing. Garyu was brave; he loved his wife and babies, but he was not strong enough to fight the evil spirits.

CHAPTER SEVEN

LOST—ONE SMALL GALEEGA

CHIEF RAYANG was gone on his expedition with Mapang and Chendang. They had taken the large boat with the carved bird on it. Dawee was up the river in the garden tending vegetables for the family. Peekew was away on some errand of his own. The village was almost empty. Cherawa knew that her father and Mapang and Peekew would not approve of Deckie's visit. But they would never know about it unless Garyu spoke, and he probably would say nothing. He was too sunk in his own wretchedness.

Then Cherawa saw the boat returning from Bukit Nyala. This time the tuan was in it, along with Deckie and Nuri. Cherawa's heart gave a bound of surprise. They were tying the canoe to the wharf. Now they were coming up the ladder. The tuan's face was grave, but he smiled at the two girls, then followed Deckie into Garyu's room. Cherawa and Jeria crowded in, too. They were eager to see what would be done now.

"Look, my friend, my brother, you are in deep trouble. We have come to help you in the name of Jesus, who sent us to this river." Deckie spoke with such kindness that Garyu raised his eyes to look again into the face of the young teacher. "Let me take the baby." Deckie reached his arms for the child. "The tuan has brought some medicine that will make the baby better. Let us try to give him a little."

Garyu hesitated for just a moment, then laid the tiny form in the outstretched arms of Deckie, who handed the little fellow to tuan. The white man seated himself on the floor and cradled the baby tenderly in his big hands.

"Get us some hot water," Deckie spoke to Cherawa, and she ran to get it. The kettle over the coals was still hot, and she was back in a minute with the hot water.

The girls watched Deckie mix the water with some thick, white fluid, which he took from one of those containers Cherawa had now learned were called "tins." Then Deckie took a small glass tube with a squeezer at the end of it. He drew up a few drops of the white fluid and dropped it very slowly into the baby's mouth. The little fellow swallowed it with listless indifference. His eyes were closed, and he seemed more dead than alive. Still he continued to swallow the medicine. Deckie did not give him much.

Garyu had watched every move of the young teacher with keen interest. Now Deckie placed the baby back in his arms. Deckie looked up at the one window of the room through which the sun was shining. He went and made a mark on the floor.

"Look, Garyu, when the shadow reaches this mark, you are to give the baby more of the medicine. We will leave the dropper here so you can put it into the baby's mouth." Deckie made another mark and another. "As the shadow reaches these marks, you must give the baby more of the medicine. If you do this, he will probably live. If you can persuade your wife to take some of it, she will get better, too. The spirits have not forbidden her to take medicine, have they?"

Garyu took the things the tuan handed him and set them away on a shelf above Treesa's mat. The men left, and Jeria and Cherawa watched them cross the river to Bukit Nyala.

Someone else had seen them go. Peekew was slowly making his way up the river against the current, and he had observed the tuan with the two younger men leave Rayang Village and cross over to the new village of Bukit Nyala. Peekew tied his boat to the wharf and came up the notched log sniffing the air as though he smelled a taint in the atmosphere.

"So the strangers came again?" He looked at the two girls who cowered in the outer porch. "And what business had they in our village, with the chief gone and Mapang gone and—?" He looked so fierce that neither Jeria nor Cherawa could give an answer. He glared at them both and then went on into his room.

Rayang with Mapang and Chendang returned soon. They had killed a large deer and brought in a fine load of venison. As the custom was, they divided it among all the families of the long house, sending a portion to each door where anyone was at home.

The excitement of this unexpected good luck engrossed the attention of Peekew, who received a double portion of all such good things; but Cherawa knew that he had not forgotten the visit of the teachers from Bukit Nyala. She resolved to tell her father at once just what had happened.

Rayang looked much disturbed after Cherawa had told him about the visit to Bukit Nyala, seeing the picture of Jesus, and her request that something be done for Treesa and her baby. She omitted nothing, even reporting how Deckie had made the marks on the floor of Garyu's room so he would know when to give the baby the medicine.

"My daughter," Chief Rayang said as he looked fondly down at his cherished Cherawa, "I think it is best for you not to go to the white man's village unless you go with me. It is not good for these strangers to interfere with our customs or try to change the commands of the spirits. Have you forgotten the Naga? How do we know but a heavy curse is hanging over our village? Peekew is doing all he can to avert calamity, but we must all be careful."

"But my galeega," said Cherawa bursting into tears; "is it not a powerful charm? I thought I could go anywhere and be protected from the anger of the spirits. I thought the village could come to no harm with so powerful a charm in it."

Rayang scratched his mangy chest. "That is probably true, my child, but we must be more careful than usual."

Late that evening Deckie's dugout again made fast to the wharf at Rayang's village. This time he did not call, but came quickly up the notched log ladder. In his arms were more tins of the white medicine that would make Treesa and her baby well again.

Cherawa had been lingering near the door of Garyu and Treesa's room. She had seen Garyu feed the baby the medicine at every advance of the shadow on the floor. The little fellow lay quiet in Garyu's arms, but his breathing was more natural. On Garyu's face Cherawa detected a look of relief and a slight flickering of hope. She saw that he had persuaded Treesa to take some of the white medicine also. Treesa slept in the

Peekew, the witch doctor, forced Deckie to take his medicine away.

early evening coolness with the older baby beside her.

As Deckie entered the long house with more of the medicine in his hands, Peekew stepped from the shadows and confronted him. Peekew was a larger man than Deckie. The radiant smile on Deckie's face seemed to infuriate him—also the fact that Deckie was humming that favorite song of his, "Everybody Ought to Love Jesus."

Peekew towered over Deckie in a menacing attitude. His deep voice rang out through the village: "Be gone, you worshiper of Jesus! We have no use for your medicine or your teaching! You are endangering our whole village! No telling what revenge the spirits will take for this! Garyu and his family want no more of your medicine, or any further visits from you."

"But the baby and Treesa will die if they don't have the medicine!" Deckie stood his ground, and the pleasant look never left his face. "I only come to do them good." Deckie looked without fear into the angry face of Peekew.

"You come to change our customs and reverse the decrees of the spirits; be gone at once!"

Deckie turned and went back to his boat. Cherawa heard him pull away from the wharf, but no song came floating back. For once the radiant Deckie was too sad to sing.

Cherawa's throat tightened. Now there was no help for Treesa and the baby. "Oh, how cruel the spirits are!" she murmured in her heart, but she dared not say it aloud. The place was likely to be full of demons listening, so she would not commit her thought to audible words. She fumbled with her necklace.

A few days later Treesa's little baby died, and the mother of Mapang did some of her best wailing and shrieking. Garyu had been treated as well as could be expected. Cherawa noticed his face as he returned to the long house, and thought she could detect a strange look about him, something hidden and determined. Treesa still lay on her mat. She still breathed, but she was so thin she looked almost transparent. She was scarcely conscious of the baby's death. She had eaten nothing for thirty days except the white medicine the tuan had brought.

The sound of wailing in the river drew Cherawa with the rest of the loungers on the long house veranda to the wharf side. It was the mother of Jeria. She was alone in her dugout canoe and rowing wildly for the home wharf. Friendly hands reached out and helped make the boat fast. The agitated woman climbed out of her boat.

"Whatever has gone wrong with you?" asked a dozen voices, but she was too excited to talk. Up in the long house among her fellow villagers, with Jeria snuggling in her arms, she at last found her tongue and told her story.

"He ate the soul! He ate the soul!" she exclaimed. "He ate the soul of Treesa's baby! He did it the night before the baby died. Oh, that horrible man! He stayed out for a long while, and when he came in, there was blood all about his mouth." The terrified woman paused for breath. "I asked him whose soul he had eaten, and he refused to say a word. He lay down on his mat, and there he is now. I don't think he even knew when I left."

All the villagers listened in stupefied silence. None of them had heard of this before except Cherawa, to whom Jeria had told her suspicions a few days before. Cherawa had not spoken of it. It was not good to tell things like that. It might arouse the interest of the spirits, and Cherawa wanted above all things to avoid that and to shelter herself under the protection of her galeega. Peekew still had her necklace, Cherawa remembered as she felt for the beloved charm. Oh, well, he would return it soon. There had been much excitement over the death of the baby and the burial—and now this terrible eater of souls!

Peekew and Mapang and the chief discussed the problem with grave faces. Peekew finally pronounced that the man should be left alone for three days out in the rice field. Then Peekew himself would go to him and try to prevent his eating any more souls out of Rayang Village. Everyone felt relieved after this decision was announced, and each fell to his own tasks, so sadly interrupted.

Chendang hustled down the notched log and into his dugout. He paddled across the river to Bukit Nyala. He was not supposed to go. Rayang had forbidden Cherawa to go by herself, but Chendang was a boy, a fine, upstanding fellow. He had never been forbidden anything. He went where he chose. Cherawa watched him go with a strong wish to follow, but she dared not.

She turned to find Peekew at her elbow. He laid the necklace in her hand. "Look, Cherawa," he said in his gentle voice, "you have been a very careless girl. What with dashing up and down the ladder and all the racing about you have done over at the tuan's new village, you have lost the galeega out of your necklace. See, the little tusk is empty!"

"Oh, my galeega! My galeega!" Cherawa lifted her voice in a shrill wail. Floods of tears and spells of screaming brought the whole village to her side, but she would not be comforted. The most precious possession of her life was gone—the matchless galeega! How could she have been so careless? Why had not her father made it more secure? Now all the spirits would find her their lawful prey! Had they not given her the most powerful charm known to man, and she had lost it?

Rayang was away hunting. He had gone directly from the council over the eater of souls. He meant to investigate some kind of wild pigtrap he had set up the river. Cherawa wailed and screamed in utter abandon. Dawee tried to comfort her, with little success. When the chief returned, she was still in Dawee's arms, her whole body racked with heartbreaking sobs.

Dawee told him the story. He shook his head and asked to see the necklace. It was placed in his hand, and he examined it with extreme care, shaking his head all the while. Then he gave the necklace to Dawee and went to find Peekew, but Peekew had also gone hunting; it was reported that he would not be back until morning.

"Cherawa," the chief said as he took his daughter in his own strong arms, "do not grieve so; perhaps we can find the galeega. Or maybe we can find another one. Don't cry any more. You will break your father's heart. Come, let us cross the river and see what is going on over at Bukit Nyala."

Cherawa knew that this was a great concession for her father to make. He did not want her to go to Bukit Nyala. He did not want her to see Deckie or listen to his stories. He did not want her to see the tuan or any of the pictures, but he was desperate to please her and to ease a little the terrible grief she felt over the loss of her charm. "What a good father he is!" Cherawa told herself as she held onto his strong hand. "How much he loves me!"

They took the big boat with the carved bird on its prow and were soon skimming over the water toward the tuan's new village. Cherawa felt a little better. She dipped up water from the river and eased her aching head and eyes. By the time they tied up at the wharf, she was able to feel a lively interest in what was going on there.

Much had happened at the new village since they had last visited it. The medicine house seemed to be open. A number of boats were tied alongside the wharf. People were sitting on the little porch of the medicine house, and others were coming out. Still others were just arriving. Cherawa recognized some of them as villagers from Sidang. Some were from Biban and Sap. Many others she did not know. They climbed the steps into the medicine house.

"A peaceful evening to you, Chief Rayang," said Deckie with his wonderful smile. He came out and looked both Cherawa and her father over in a way he had never done before. "You both have the ringworm all over your bodies. Why don't you come and let us put our medicine on you so you can have good, clean, smooth skins again like this girl?" He lifted his own plump little daughter, Nancy, from the floor and perched her on his shoulder. Her soft brown skin was smooth and beautiful to see. Cherawa looked at her own scruffy, itchy arms and legs and then up into her father's face.

CHAPTER EIGHT

ONE NEW SKIN—WHAT PRICE?

"How much does it cost to have your medicine and this new skin you are talking about?" Chief Rayang asked Teacher Deckie.

"We ask everyone who gets medicine from us to bring two coconut shells full of rice." Deckie sounded very businesslike. "But I warn you, the medicine will hurt! It burns like fire the first two or three times it is put on, but after that it scarcely hurts at all. Isn't that true, Nuri?"

Nuri held out his arms, to which the medicine had just been applied. It left a slight deposit of white on the skin, which was still rough and scruffy. "Mine doesn't hurt any more," Nuri said with a smile, "but it sure hurt plenty the first time!"

Cherawa looked in through the open door of the medicine house. There was a row of people standing in front of the counter, seven or eight of them. The tuan had a large can in his hand, also a brush with which he was painting the arms and legs and bodies of the people. They could not bear to have the hot medicine painted all over them at once, so the tuan began at one end of the line and treated an arm for each one. As the medicine was applied, the men and women would blow on it and dance a little for a few seconds. Then they would quiet down and wait for the tuan to begin over and do the other arm.

Five or six times the tuan went down the row applying the medicine. Once he stopped and filled his can from a very large one which was sitting behind the counter. It took lots of medicine. Cherawa and Chief Rayang said nothing for a long time.

"Would you like to try the medicine?" asked Deckie of Rayang. "I am not sure Cherawa can stand it. So far no children have been brave enough to stand the pain of the first two or three treatments."

"Oh, Father!" Cherawa caught her father's hand. "Please, Father, I want to try the medicine! I want a good skin. I don't care how much it hurts. Let me try! Please let me try!"

"I have no rice to pay you," Rayang explained. Cherawa could see that her father wanted to please her on account of the galeega. She would have to come back again and again for the medicine. She would get to know all about what was going on here at Bukit

Nyala. She would have a chance to hear more about Jesus and—she would be willing to endure any pain for that!

"You can bring a double amount next time you come." Deckie laid his hand on Rayang's shoulder. "You will have to come every second day for a while, and you will have to keep coming about two moons in order to be completely cured."

Rayang and Cherawa stepped into the waiting line. Before long the tuan had finished with the first line of patients, and the second group stood before the counter. The tuan applied the hot medicine to Rayang's arm. He did not flinch or manifest any evidence of pain at all. Then the tuan drew Cherawa's skinny arm out to its full length. There was a look of great kindness on his face as he slowly applied the medicine. It hurt! The itching scruffy skin turned red and angry. It felt like fire! But Cherawa did not make any demonstration. She did not dance or blow her breath on her arm, but waited quietly for the tuan to come back and do the other arm.

The tuan was speaking to Deckie. He took a little tight bag and a round package out from behind the long counter.

"Cherawa," Deckie said as he came toward her, "the tuan says you are the first little girl he has ever seen who is brave enough to take the ringworm medicine without crying. He wants to give you a present." Deckie placed the two packages in Cherawa's hands. "Please come back the day after tomorrow for another treatment."

Rayang and Cherawa were not yet ready to leave the medicine house. There was too much to see and hear. They loitered on the porch.

Cherawa was very much surprised to see the wife of Sawa climbing the steep path. The poor old lady was thin and bony. The sky had become cloudy, and rain was beginning to fall. The wife of Sawa shivered in the cool air. Her body was naked except for the short skirt worn by all the women of her tribe.

"Tuan, tuan!" the wife of Sawa pleaded, "my bones are aching. Can you rub me again with the hot medicine?"

The wife of Sawa was a regular visitor at the medicine house. Cherawa watched the tuan apply the rubbing medicine to the old woman's swollen joints and heard her exclamations of pain and satisfaction. The hot oil seemed to comfort her. When she was about to leave, the tuan took a package from under the counter, opened it, and displayed a garment of such beauty and soft warmth that everyone in the medicine house came to examine it.

It was a jacket of fuzzy, soft material, white as the kapok fluff. The tuan took it out and smiled. "Here,

Mother," he addressed the wife of Sawa, "my wife has made this warm jacket for you. She feels sorry that you are always cold and shivering and aching. If you will wear this, it will keep you warm, and you will feel better."

The old woman could not grasp the meaning of the tuan's broken talk. He came round the counter and slipped her skinny arms into the jacket, buttoning it over her hollow chest.

"For you! For you!" he shouted at her, and all the rest of the visitors at the medicine house recovered from their astonishment enough to chime in a chorus, "For you, Mother, for you! It is the tuan's wife who sent it to you to keep you warm."

With a look of blank astonishment the old woman scurried down the path to her boat. Cherawa could see her paddling with wild strokes toward her own village. The white jacket glistened in the river like a point of light.

"So that tuan has a wife?" Rayang questioned Nuri, who had come down to the landing place with them.

"Yes, he has a wife and some children, both sons and daughters. He is going to build a house on the very top of the hill of Nyala, and when it is done, he will bring his family to live at this place."

"Why do they come here, Nuri?" Rayang asked

the youth. "Surely they would be more comfortable in their own country among their own people and friends."

"It is for love of the man Jesus they have come," Nuri explained. "This man Jesus wants people everywhere to know and love Him and worship Him."

Rayang shook his head. "It must be that many years ago their fathers and our fathers had some dealings, and they feel they owe us some kind of debt."

"That may be," Nuri replied as he considered the idea; "that may be. I have heard Deckie say he was debtor to all men. Maybe you are right."

At the landing place other Ibans loitered. They were waiting for Nuri. They sat on their heels and chewed betel nut and questioned Nuri about all the recent doings at Bukit Nyala. Nuri repeated what he had just told Chief Rayang. "These people are here because of love to this man Jesus. This Jesus has given command for all men everywhere to worship Him."

"What? Worship Him instead of the spirits?" an eager voice queried.

"Yes," Nuri continued, "since Tuan Allah made everything, all people and everything else, I guess He would have a right to command people to worship His Son."

This was startling information. Everyone chewed for a few minutes, thinking it over.

"Tuan Allah is king of all the stars and the sun, and He has made His Son Jesus to be king of this world, so it looks like we should worship Him."

It was too wonderful for Cherawa to understand. Her mind seemed bursting with a great desire to contain all this wonderful knowledge, but it was too much for her. She only knew that something warm and comforting seemed to be wrapped about her. She felt safe at Bukit Nyala. This was no place for evil spirits. They were not likely to stay around where this Jesus person was so much loved and respected. The terrible loss of the galeega did not seem so bad as it had over on the other side of the river at the home village.

As they untied the dugout, Cherawa wondered about Chendang. She had not seen him all day. He had been crossing the river to Bukit Nyala when she last saw him. Cherawa suspected that Chendang had become rather a close friend of Nuri and Deckie. He was eleven years old, almost twelve. He was a bright boy and could row a boat and hunt and fish like a grown man. He knew many things, and Cherawa had respect for his judgment. However, he was willful and self-reliant. Neither of his parents made any effort to direct his activities beyond making kind suggestions now and then. It appeared to Cherawa that he did exactly as he pleased all the time. She often regretted that she had not been born a boy.

CHAPTER NINE

THE BELIEVERS

"I TOLD them all about the eater of souls," Chendang whispered to his sister as they sat together in the outer veranda of the long house. "I told them about Treesa's baby dying and how the father of Jeria had eaten its soul."

It was the evening after Rayang and Cherawa had taken their first ringworm treatment, the same day that Cherawa had found out that her galeega was lost. She had cried herself out. "There are no more tears in my eyes," she told Chendang. He had a number of secrets to tell her, so the two had crept off to a secluded corner behind a pile of kajang, the leafy sheets of dried palm thatch of which walls were often made.

"What did Deckie and the tuan say when you told them about the baby's soul being eaten?" Cherawa was much interested.

"They asked me to go with them to Jeria's father.

They didn't know where his garden was, of course," Chendang continued.

"Oh, Chendang! Did you take them there?" Cherawa was suddenly terrified at what her brother had done.

"Of course I took them there. How else would they know the way? We found him still on his mat. He was very pale and weak and couldn't talk much. The tuan and Deckie say he has the lung sickness, so that when he coughs, blood comes up out of his mouth. They gave him food and drink and some of that white medicine they wanted to give Treesa."

"So he didn't eat the baby's soul after all." Cherawa was relieved, much relieved.

"No, of course not. He was sick, and he didn't want to worry and frighten his wife, so he would get up from his sleeping mat and go outside when he felt the coughing coming on." Chendang paused for breath in his rapid telling of the story. "The tuan says he will not live long. They went twice to see him yesterday, and they talked a long time to him about Jesus. It seems that Jesus loves just anybody, and all those who believe in Him can be taken up to His home somewhere in the sky. They will never be sick or sad. They will never be hungry or suffer anything any more."

"Oh, Chendang! And you went with them?" Cherawa spoke in an awed voice.

"I love that Jesus Man," Chendang went on in a softer voice. "I feel all warm and happy inside since I told Deckie that I'm not going to worship the spirits any more. I am just going to belong to Jesus, and He will take care of me."

Something vibrant, with a joy that was almost pain, coursed through Cherawa's body. Both children sat still for a long time.

Then voices arose near them. It was Peekew and their father, the chief. They heard the chief's voice, high and insistent. "But you know the galeega was securely fastened. I made doubly sure of that. I have examined the necklace every morning and every evening since Cherawa has been wearing it. It has never been loosened in any way."

A long silence followed. Then the musical voice of Peekew spoke out of the darkness: "The chief of Rayang is a very stupid man," he remarked. "Can you not see that both your children are infected with this Jesus teaching? Can you not understand that to leave a powerful spirit charm in the hand of one whose heart is already estranged from the spirits is a most dangerous thing? It may bring untold calamity on this village and on your own house and children. I took what I felt was the kindest way to place the galeega where it belongs."

Cherawa's heart almost stopped beating, then

started pounding. She put her hand over her chest to still its noise, lest the two men hear it in the darkness and seek her out. Chendang was as shocked as Cherawa.

The chief and Peekew argued a little more about the charm. Then both men withdrew and sought their sleeping mats. Cherawa and Chendang still lingered in the darkness, not daring to come out until the moon rose high in the heavens. Then they leaned over the railing and gazed out into the night.

Down the stream, a little way below the wharf, they saw a boat put in. Both children strained their eyes to see who might be making a furtive return to Rayang late at night. The lone rower carried a bundle in his hand. With stealthy footsteps he came up the notched log into the village. It was Garyu!

"He goes to take the white medicine from the tuan secretly," whispered Chendang. "Have you noticed that Treesa is getting stronger? Garyu listens to the Jesus teaching every night. Then he comes home and tells Treesa all he hears at Bukit Nyala."

"And does Treesa believe it?" Cherawa breathed the question.

"I don't think she knows whether she believes or not." Chendang sat down on his heels again. "She is so weak. She just clings to Garyu and does what he says. Sometimes she is very frightened of the spirits. Then Garyu holds her in his arms and whispers the name of Jesus over and over again. It is a powerful charm to her. She becomes quiet and rests."

So Chendang had heard all this at Bukit Nyala. Cherawa shuddered at the thought of what would happen if the secret visits of Garyu to Bukit Nyala were discovered. Both children sat on their heels a little longer meditating on the secrets that had been revealed to them that night. Then, without more talk, they went to bed. Dawee and Rayang had not slept. They were talking about the galeega when the two children came into the room. Now they became silent.

The next day Peekew, Mapang, and the chief of Rayang went to visit the father of Jeria. He had been alone for the three days Peekew had prescribed. They would see if he was in a better mood. Perhaps they could win him away from his practice of eating souls. Chendang went with them. Cherawa watched them go. She knew that Peekew had her galeega. It was among his charms. He would probably use it on Jeria's father.

"It is my galeega!" Cherawa gritted her teeth and shook her fist at the departing medicine man. "He had no right to steal it!" She said these awful words aloud, but nobody heard. The women were all busy with weaving and cooking. Even Jeria's mother seemed to take little interest in the condition of her soul-eating husband.

The rice supply was now low in the village, and the people had nothing of value which they were willing to trade for rice from the other villages. Cherawa heard Dawee say that they had rice enough for one more week; then they would have to eat ferns from the jungle, tapioca root, or sago. Cherawa loathed sago above all other food. She would much rather starve than eat sago. She thought about it now and resolved that she would never eat sago again. She would die first.

Dawee called her to help with the weaving, and Cherawa was soon busy with her usual village tasks. All the time she was listening for the sound of oars in the river. She remembered that today was the day for another treatment for the ringworm.

The men had taken Rayang's large boat with the carved bird. Cherawa saw it when it rounded the curve of the river. There was something unusual about its appearance. As it came nearer, she saw that the boat contained a large, well-wrapped bundle. It was the body of Jeria's father! He had died of the coughing sickness. She could not speak a word. Soon the whole village was running together and shrieking and wailing in the manner Cherawa remembered so well.

Chendang gave his sister the whole story as soon as they had a moment alone. "We found him dead on his mat," Chendang said in a sad voice, "but there was a warm blanket over him and food at his elbow. Deckie and the tuan had been there."

"Did Peekew and Mapang know?" Cherawa asked in a low voice.

"Yes, they knew that someone had visited him, and they recognized the blanket as one of Deckie's."

"Oh, Chendang, do you suppose they were with him when he died?"

"I shouldn't wonder," Chendang replied. "The last time I came with them the sick man told them that he believed in Jesus because the love of Jesus had sent Deckie to show him kindness in his dying hour."

"Peekew doesn't know that, of course?" Cherawa wanted to be sure.

"No, he doesn't know that, but he knows enough so he is sulky and cross."

"Oh, Chendang, I am afraid my father will not be willing to take me to Bukit Nyala to get ringworm medicine this day!"

Cherawa was not long in suspense. She saw her father tie up a quantity of rice in an old loincloth; he motioned her to come with the party who were proceeding to the burial place to administer the last rites to Jeria's father.

Poor little Jeria was taken in the boat with them and sat sobbing with Cherawa's arm around her all through the sickening experience. Jeria's mother, being a devotee of the spirits and a good wailer in her own right, went in the boat with Indai Mapang, and the two women made the trip hideous with their cries and moans.

On the return journey the chief directed his boat toward Bukit Nyala. They appeared at the medicine house just as the sun was going down. It hung in the heavens over the great range of wooded hills like a ball of fire.

Deckie was just closing up the medicine house. "It is almost time for Tuan Allah's rest day to begin." He smiled at them. "There will just be time for me to apply your medicine." He painted the hot medicine on their bodies with skill and with as much speed as they could bear. Neither father nor daughter gave any evidence of suffering, although the medicine felt exceedingly hot and painful. It didn't hurt quite so much as the first time. Rayang turned in his bag of rice, which Deckie emptied into a large bin behind the counter. Many people must be coming for medicine. There was plenty of rice in the bin.

"What do you mean by Tuan Allah's rest day?" asked Rayang of Deckie when the medicine was given and they were ready to return to their boat.

"When Tuan Allah made the world, He made it in six days. He saw that everything He had made was beautiful and good, so He rested on the seventh day because He had finished His beautiful work, and because He wanted to remember His great love to man and how well He provided everything for man's happiness. You see He had made all the plans so man could rest in the love of Tuan Allah."

The chief grunted as he always did when he could not understand, or when he wanted time to think things over. Together father and daughter went to the dugout and, in the glorious sunset, made their way across the river to the home village.

Before going into her own room, Cherawa looked in at Garyu's door. Treesa was sitting on her mat. She smiled at Cherawa. Although she was still thin and wasted, it was evident to any observant person that she was getting a little better. There was a bowl of rice in Garyu's hand. It looked to Cherawa as though Treesa had been eating some of the rice.

"Look, Cherawa," Garyu said as he motioned her toward them, "you are a friend of the tuan and Deckie, and you have heard of Jesus." Cherawa nodded in solemn agreement. "I am a believer in this Jesus. I don't know much about Him yet, but I do know that He loves us and has sent help to us. If we could have received the help He sent us sooner, our baby need not have died. You see, Treesa is getting better." Garyu smiled with warm affection at his wife. He leaned toward Cherawa and whispered in a soft voice, "The

Cherawa looked out over the flowing river and thought about Jesus.

name of Jesus is a powerful charm. When you are in trouble, say it over and over again, and your heart will find comfort and security."

Treesa did not say anything, but she nodded her head and smiled again. Cherawa left the room filled with wonder and fear, and a strange tumult of joy filled her heart. Chendang was a believer, and Nuri surely was too. And now Garyu and Treesa! Was she also a believer? Cherawa looked out over the dark-flowing river and up to the star-sprinkled heavens and asked of her heart the great question. But she could not answer. The song of Deckie sang an accompaniment of harmony to the struggle in her soul—"Everybody Ought to Love Jesus." He died on the cross to save us from sin. What was the cross, and what was sin? And why would Jesus die for people He had never seen or known? No, there were too many questions. She could not follow so far—not yet.

In the morning Cherawa and Chendang were up early. "I'm going to get some green coconuts for Deckie," Chendang announced as he led the way to the tall coconut tree behind the long house.

He leaned his beloved knife against the base of the tree trunk and prepared for the climb. It was a tall tree and not often climbed. The wind sometimes blew the ripe nuts down, and they were gathered by the villagers; but the tree did not bear much fruit.

Fearless Chendang slowly inched his way up the tall coconut tree.

Cherawa watched Chendang inch his way up the rough trunk of the tree. At the top he loosened all the nuts that were fully grown. There were not many. Cherawa circled around out of range of the falling nuts.

Then Chendang started to slide down, slowly at first, but his arms seemed to be getting tired and numb. As he got to the middle of the tree, he began to slide faster and faster.

"Hold on tight! Hold on tight!" Cherawa screeched at him, but it was no use. Down he came with all his weight, and neither of them remembered the knife standing point upwards at the base of the tree!

"Ayoh! Ayoh!" Cherawa's screams brought every person in the long house running. Nearly everyone was there, for it was still early morning. Chendang lay on the ground under the tree. The knife had gone clear through the inside of his thigh and stuck out several inches. He was bleeding furiously. His father bent over him. Mapang removed the knife.

"Take me to Deckie! Take me to Deckie!" Chendang screamed with every breath.

With a hard look at Peekew, Rayang gathered his son in his arms and raced for his boat. Peekew and Mapang followed in Mapang's boat. Cherawa and Dawee raced along in the little dugout.

The passage of the river had probably never been managed in so short a time. The boats stayed close together. None wanted to be left behind. Cherawa heard Peekew say to Mapang, "I told Rayang that a curse is on his house because of his children listening to this Jesus teaching. His daughter was even wearing the galeega in her necklace and running after this new belief."

Mapang scowled but he did not speak. He was in the prow of his boat where he could see Cherawa. He knew how sharp her ears were. Then they were at the wharf. The chief had already carried Chendang, now very quiet, up to the medicine house. Deckie and the tuan were kneeling beside him trying to stop the flow of blood.

Chendang was still conscious. He looked up into the faces of Deckie and the tuan with such love and confidence that Cherawa could not stifle the scream in her throat. No one paid any attention to her.

Under the efforts of the two men the flow of blood ceased, and they began bandaging the wound with clean white cloth.

"He should not move his leg for several hours." Deckie explained what the tuan was saying. "He must stay right here on this mat until tomorrow. Then he can probably go home. Some of you should stay with him. We believe he will be all right. It seems to be a clean wound. It has bled a great deal. He is weak, but he will be all right in a few days."

These comforting words were passed around among the large crowd that had gathered in front of the medicine house. People began to depart. Peekew and Mapang withdrew with sullen faces and crossed the river to Rayang village.

Cherawa begged to be allowed to stay with her brother. The chief, after assuring himself that his son was being well cared for and would recover, told Cherawa and Dawee to remain there, and he returned to the village, promising to bring their sleeping mats before nightfall.

So it came to pass that the wife and children of Chief Rayang spent a day and a night at the new village of Bukit Nyala.

CHAPTER TEN

THE MEDICINE HOUSE

IN THE little back room of the medicine house Chendang lay on his mat. His mother and sister watched beside him, so wakeful that they could not rest although their mats were prepared.

They were not alone. Deckie sat cross-legged beside Chendang. When he roused from sleep, as he often did, Deckie gave him water from a pitcher at his side. Chendang drank with eager lips, then reached for Deckie's hand. And with a sigh of deep content he slept again.

No one spoke. It was important that the wounded boy be disturbed as little as possible. Cherawa studied the face of Deckie. Candlelight cast a faint glow over everything, and in that shadowed light the face of Deckie seemed to have some quality of inner illumination, alight with something apart from the faint shining of the candle.

Even in his sleep the face of Chendang seemed to have taken on something of the radiant peace that shone in the face of the older boy who leaned over him with such tenderness.

When the sun rose over Biban, Chendang sat up with a smile, and Deckie patted him on the shoulder. "You have done well, Chendang; now just don't move around too much today, and by this evening you should be able to go home."

Then Deckie departed for his own room in Sidang Village to get a little rest. The tuan came down from the hill where he had been laying out the plan for his own house, and the medicine house came to life.

"Peekew and Mapang will say now that the curse of the Naga has fallen on our family." Dawee spoke in confidence to Cherawa.

"Naga! Naga!" exclaimed Chendang, rising on his elbow; "I must tell you about the Naga. You know I told Deckie about the Naga, and one day about a moon ago Deckie and I went up Sungi Sap to find the Naga. Deckie said he had no fear of Nagas, and of course I wasn't afraid with Deckie."

"Oh, Chendang, did you see it?" Cherawa clasped her hands in wonder.

"We saw where the Naga had been," continued Chendang. "We saw the pair of branching horns on the river bank and the dry place where he had lain long enough so that the grass was dead under him."

Dawee and Cherawa were almost speechless with amazement. Chendang laughed at their round eyes and went on with his story. "Deckie examined everything, and he told me that the Naga was just an ordinary python like the one that frightened you when you were lost that time." He stopped to see his words take effect. "Deckie says the python had swallowed a deer. Of course he couldn't swallow the horns, so they just stuck out of his mouth until the carcass digested and the horns fell off on the sand."

Cherawa turned this revelation over in her mind for a full minute. She remembered how the Naga's eyes were above the horns. When she considered it in the light of Chendang's explanation, it did seem reasonable.

"I saw it myself!" she exclaimed. "I saw it myself, and I do believe Deckie is right. The snake was no bigger than the one I found in the bamboo, and he must have swallowed a deer. Of course it was the horns that made him look so unusual. How stupid of us not to know!"

"When people believe in Jesus," Chendang pointed out, "it takes away fear and enlightens them. They can see clearly and understand better. The worship of the spirits fills us with such fright that we can see nothing in its true shape, so the forest is full of fearful things." Chendang lay back on his mat exhausted, still weak from loss of blood the day before.

Dawee and Cherawa had been instructed to give him all the water he could be induced to drink. The tuan, who was getting on a little with his study of the native language, invited Dawee to cook rice for the children. He took a kettle and fish and vegetables from his own kitchen. Within an hour the meal was ready.

Nuri had been sent from Sidang by Deckie to take his place at the medicine house. The visitors had already started coming. A line of five or six already stood waiting for the hot ringworm medicine. Cherawa stepped into line. This was her third treatment. Already the fire of the medicine was dulled. It no longer stung and burned as it did at first. Her skin was more dry and scruffy, but less irritable.

Rain began and fell in torrents. New arrivals scampered into the river house to wait until the worst of the shower was over, but to Cherawa's surprise the mother of Sawa made her way up the hill in the driving rain. She held a banana leaf over her head as a slight protection.

She had come for the hot rubbing medicine, and she asked the tuan to put the hot oil on her joints, as she was racked with pains and aches.

"But, Mother," said tuan, slowly picking his words as he spoke, "where is the new jacket I gave you last time you were here? This is just the kind of day when you should wear it. It would keep you warm and make you feel better."

The poor old woman turned an astonished face on the white man. "What, wear that jacket in the rain!" she exclaimed. "I am saving that jacket to be buried in."

"Look," said Nuri, "that is what's the matter with us all. We are saving the comfort of God to be buried in instead of being warm and safe in it right now."

But Cherawa did not comprehend what Nuri meant by "the comfort of God." It must be something he had learned from Deckie.

"Is it true that the tuan is building a house on top of the hill?" Dawee inquired of her son.

"The Chinese are leveling it now. Why don't you go and see? I go every day." Chendang motioned his mother and sister away.

They climbed the many steps to the top of the hill. A number of men were busy making a flat floor of the earth. The place seemed very large. "I wonder how big the house is going to be."

"Look, Mother, see the stakes with little white rags on them? I think those are the markings showing where the walls of the house will be." Cherawa spoke out of experience. She had seen similar stakes on the sites where the river house and the medicine house now stood.

"Then it will be a large house. The tuan must have many children and many servants." Dawee turned back.

"Mother, what do you think about this Jesus who sends these people here? Do you think He should be worshiped instead of the spirits?" For the first time Cherawa dared to face her mother with the great question.

"Child, I don't know; these people are so kind. Whoever sent them must be kind, too. The spirits are not kind."

Cherawa's heart lifted like a flower in the morning sunshine. Her mother—her quiet little mother—was also friendly to Jesus! She skipped down the hill humming the now beloved song "Everybody Ought to Love Jesus."

The rain, which had ceased for a half hour, now began again. There seemed to be unusual excitement at the wharf. Cherawa saw a man being carried through the pelting rain to the medicine house. She and Dawee hastened their steps and arrived about the same time as the new patient. The man was terribly wounded. His shoulder was mangled in a frightful way, and the whole muscle of his left leg was torn away and hung loose. However, the wounded parts were so swollen that there was little bleeding.

"He was caught by a crocodile last night," the men

who had brought him explained. "He was fishing and the crocodile overturned his boat. He fought and got away, but you see he is nine tenths a dead man. We rowed all night against the tide to bring him to you."

Nuri was sent to boil a lot of water. The tuan bent over the man, examining his frightful wounds.

"He will die of course," said one onlooker.

"Why do they bring a dead man here?" asked another.

The man, who was fully conscious, looked up with fear into the face of the white man. Then the tuan spoke in his broken talk. "Do not be afraid, brother. The man Jesus who directs everything about this place is strong and kind. Just rest and don't worry."

Cherawa watched the tuan put large wet compresses on the swollen wounded leg and shoulder. The man relaxed and was soon asleep. His wounds were not bandaged. The compresses were changed every half hour. At noon Deckie returned and took up his duties at the medicine house.

All day the people came. Some had headaches; some had stomach-aches. Many came for the ringworm medicine. Some came who were in terrible need. Toward evening there came a man whose hand was so swollen that the skin seemed in danger of bursting. "I was gathering shoots of wild fern in the jungle, and a snake took hold of my hand," he explained.

All day long the people came to be healed at the medicine house.

His hand was treated to reduce the swelling and pain. Then it was lanced to allow the poisoned blood to escape. The man was invited to stay for the night so that his hand might be treated in the morning, but he refused. "I live far away, and I must return home," he said. "I am sure the hand will recover now. I have no pain, and peace is in my heart."

There also came a youth who was in utter agony with a solid mass of tiny boils all over the front of his body. "I was sliding down a tree and slid through a mass of poison caterpillars," he explained. The poor fellow was taken in charge by Deckie who poulticed the boils, soothing the lad all the while with comforting words.

At sundown Rayang came to take his family home. He brought several sticks of eggs; the eggs were wrapped one by one in a long leaf. The leaf was stiff, and when the whole was wrapped, it looked like a lumpy stick. He also brought two chickens, for Rayang was truly grateful for what had been done for his son. The rice was now so low in the bin at home that he could no longer bring rice. So he pressed these offerings on Deckie, who received them with smiles and thanks.

Nuri and Deckie lifted Chendang between them and carried him to his father's boat.

"Just keep him quiet; he will be all right," Deckie

admonished the chief as they pulled away from shore.

During the time she had been at Bukit Nyala, Cherawa had thought often of her galeega, but somehow at Bukit Nyala it seemed unimportant to have a powerful charm. Now as they pulled up at the home wharf, all the weight of grief over her loss came back, and she began weeping aloud.

"Be patient, my daughter," Chief Rayang spoke with sadness, "be patient; you shall have your charm again. I will surely get it for you. Trust your father, child."

Thus comforted, Cherawa reduced her wailing to sobs and climbed the notched log into the village. The sun had set and night had come, for in that country night follows day abruptly, with little twilight between. Chendang was taken to his sleeping mat, and Cherawa went to sit for a moment with Treesa and Garyu. Her face was still wet with tears and her eyes red from her recent weeping.

"Oh, Cherawa," exclaimed Treesa with a bright smile, "how wonderful that Chendang is better! We were both afraid that he would die. Peekew and Mapang said he would surely never get well because the Naga was angry with Rayang for allowing you children to listen to the Jesus teaching."

Then Treesa saw that Cherawa had been crying. "What are you sad about, little sister? This is a day of gladness. Just think, Chendang might have been dead had it not been for Deckie and the tuan."

There was such kindness in Treesa's voice that Cherawa felt herself comforted. She told Treesa and Garyu the whole sad story of her galeega: how her father had found it, how he had worked for days to make her the beautiful necklace, and how he had concealed the galeega in the boar's tusk. She told how Peekew came to have knowledge of the charm, and how he had borrowed the necklace and removed the galeega. She told of the conversation she had overheard between her father and Peekew.

Treesa and Garyu listened to the sad tale with grave interest. "I guess we were so buried in our own troubles we didn't hear about yours, although I do remember your father quieting the frightened villagers that night with your necklace." Garyu spoke with sympathy. "Of course it was wrong for Peekew to take your charm, but it is not so powerful a charm as the name of Jesus," Garyu continued with much conviction. "The name of Jesus has power to drive away the evil spirits and to make your heart as light as the white clouds floating above the river."

Garyu smiled and Cherawa studied his face. A great peace seemed to have settled over the room of Garyu and Treesa. It sat on their two faces. It enfolded her too. She realized with a start that Treesa was looking much better. In the frail light of the candle her face still looked pale, but her cheeks had filled out, and her voice was stronger.

"It is good to hear you say that the name of Jesus is a powerful charm." Cherawa measured every word.

"I want Jesus, but I want my galeega, too."

It was still early. Cherawa was not sleepy. Her mind was full of active thoughts. The terrible itching of the ringworm all over her body had lessened until an unusual sense of well-being enveloped her. She stretched her legs and twisted her head. Missing were the itching, the pain, the scratching, and the dried blood where sharp fingernails had clawed the scruffy skin! "I am growing a new skin," she said to herself, "a good one, too, this time. Of course it is all because this Jesus Man sent tuan and Deckie to this river."

Then her thoughts went to the Naga. She pondered over the revelation Chendang had made. In her heart she knew it must be true. The Naga was just an ordinary snake, magnified into a thing of terror by the witch doctor. She thought about the results of the fear that had oppressed the village on account of the Naga: the ban had been laid on the village; the rice fields had been neglected and ruined; the village was facing famine right now; Garyu's father had died; Treesa's baby had died—all might have been so different. Now it was too late.

CHAPTER ELEVEN

TERCOOP OR HEAVEN

THE rain was falling in torrents. The noise of the wind in the trees and the rattle of loose shakes on the roof obliterated all lesser sounds. It was a night to snuggle inside a cozy room with friends.

The violence of the rainstorm concealed a stealthy creeping of footsteps across the floor of what had been the room of Garyu's father. It was deserted now. Both of the old folk had died. Since nobody wanted to take up quarters in a dead man's room, it stood empty. Who would venture into such a room in the dark night? The spirit of the departed might reach out and clutch you from the wall. Long fingers might descend from the high ceiling and lift you right out through the roof. Who indeed dare enter?

The next room belonged to Peekew. He sat that night with all his charms spread out on a fine mat

Peekew, the witch doctor, spread his charms on the mat before him.

before him. He had barred the door, so that there would be no danger of visitors entering unannounced. On the mat were a small dried crocodile, a powerful stimulant, and a pale white skeleton of a sea bird, which was useful in determining favorable times for marrying and planting. Peekew also had an elephant tooth acquired in trade with a Punan witch doctor and the skull of an okang, a slothlike creature of the jungle. He looked at a sedative charm which worked in many difficult cases, then at the master charm, a cluster of black seeds with a high polish used to determine the outcome of illness. Next he gazed at a varied assortment of herbs, bones, teeth, and hair. But Peekew held something tenderly in his hand.

"Ah, what indeed?" inquired Cherawa with her keen eye pressed to a small hole in the wall between the two rooms.

It was Chendang, of course, who conceived the plan. Cherawa longed to see with her own eyes the galeega in the hands of the witch doctor. She had disclosed her wish to Chendang; and Chendang, bold in his new-found safety in the Jesus teaching, had no fear of ghosts in the deserted room of Garyu's dead father. On this stormy night, when a heavy footfall could not be heard, Peekew did not suspect that he was being watched through two peek holes newly opened in his wall.

"Charm of all charms," the witch doctor addressed the small irregular stone in his hand. His thin lips parted in a satisfied smile. His egg-shaped head nodded in great content. "With this I will chase the Jesus teaching from this river!" He held the stone between his fingers and lifted it so the light from the candle glowed on it. Sucking in his breath with delight, he placed the galeega carefully in the bottom of his betel nut box.

"Oh, Chendang! What do you think he will do with my galeega?" Cherawa inquired in an excited voice after the children had crept back to the inner veranda of the long house.

"He is up to some mischief." Chendang shook his head. "Hard to tell what he is planning. We must keep our eyes open. I don't think he will try another ban. The last one only did harm. All the village feel that they would have had a fine rice crop this season had it not been for that cursed Naga and Peekew's ban."

"Tomorrow you must tell Deckie," Cherawa spoke after a thoughtful pause; "you must tell him that Peekew has stolen the most powerful charm known to the Ibans, and he intends to use it to do them harm and drive them from this river."

"I do not think they are in grave danger," Chendang mused with a faint smile on his handsome face; "I can't imagine either Deckie or the tuan being scared of a piece of stone cut out of a dead monkey's liver."

The two children crept along under the clusters of heads to their own door. "I will tell Deckie in the morning," Chendang promised just before they opened the heavy door to their own room and sought their sleeping mats. Cherawa felt with a twinge of terror that Chendang had ceased to regard any of the village superstitions with any reverence at all. It worried her, and yet—he might be right!

Every day Chendang went across the river to have his wound dressed. It was almost healed now. Cherawa had gone every other day for her ringworm treatment. The scruffy skin was falling from her body in patches. Her legs and arms were almost clean of the ringworm. There was no longer any pain connected with the treatment; the medicine felt cool and puckery on her new skin. The chief of Rayang was looking different, too. His skin had cleared rapidly, and everyone remarked on the change. He was a fine-looking fellow now. Dozens of other people were recovering from their skin ailment. Up and down the river new skins were the style.

"I have had nine skins and lost them all. Now I have a good one at last," said the woman next in line to Cherawa as she stood waiting the next morning in the medicine house.

"I can sleep for the first time in my life," remarked

her friend. "I scratched myself all my life until now."

After Deckie had dressed Chendang's wound, he motioned to both the children. "Come and see the hens. The tuan just brought them over yesterday." He led the way to a newly devised chicken pen where a couple dozen enormous red hens picked at the rice scattered about on the ground.

"I have a present for you if you can receive it." Deckie laughed. He brought from the medicine house a small basket. It contained eight eggs. To the eyes of Cherawa and Chendang the great brown eggs in the basket looked like something unreal.

"Teacher Deckie," said Chendang, drawing in his breath with a deep sigh, "those just can't be hen eggs! They look like the eggs of the Naga!" At that both Deckie and Chendang laughed with such hearty mirth that Cherawa was afraid. She knew they were both thinking of the same thing: the horrid hoax that had been foisted on Rayang's village by Peekew and Mapang over the big swamp python that had swallowed a deer. But was it safe to laugh about such things? Perhaps it was safe at Bukit Nyala. Certainly neither Deckie nor Chendang had the least fear in the matter.

"The eggs are for you, Chendang." Deckie put the basket in his hand. "But you will have to find a hen to hatch them for you. None of our hens are broody."

"We are just clearing for our new rice field, and I

will take them out to our garden. We have a few hens out there who are always broody. But what do you suppose those hens will think when they see such eggs as these?" Chendang laughed again.

"I think any hen should be proud to sit on them," Deckie answered. "Take them and see."

Chendang put the basket of eggs in the boat and spread several thicknesses of banana leaf over them to keep them cool. Deckie had gone back to his duties in the medicine house, but neither Cherawa nor Chendang was ready to leave Bukit Nyala. They wanted to talk more.

"Teacher Deckie,"—Chendang laid his hand on Deckie's arm during a lull in his ministry to patients —"do the souls all go into the tercoop?" Chendang asked the question with an earnest face.

"What do you mean, Chendang?" Deckie asked. "Come and show me what you mean. There is plenty of tercoop growing down by the river house where the tuan lives."

Chendang led the way down the hill. "Look," he said, breaking off a stalk of reed grass and holding it out for Deckie to see, "you can see the blood inside." The stalk was hollow and suffused with a red color like blood.

"Our people say that the souls of the Ibans all go into the tercoop. That is why they are red inside."

Chendang broke off several more stalks. Some were green inside; others were like the first one, blood red.

"You see, teacher," Chendang said as he looked sadly at the stalk he was holding, "there are some tercoop stalks still empty, but in time they will all be full. When enough Ibans die, they will all be full."

"Look, Chendang," Deckie replied, pronouncing every word with force, "do you think the great Tuan Allah who made you so strong and happy and full of life wants you to end up in a stalk of tercoop? Does it seem reasonable to you?" Deckie took the stalk of reed into his own hand. "The reason why this red color is here is because a small insect has stung this stalk and poisoned it, so it turned red. It has nothing at all to do with the souls of the Ibans. Come, I will ask you something."

Deckie led the two children to a place behind the medicine house where some digging was going on. He seized a heavy grub hoe and began chopping into the bank. In a few minutes he found what he sought. He chopped into a white root. It was almost as thick as a child's wrist, but easily cut, and from the cut surface there oozed drops of what looked like blood. It congealed almost at once.

"Tell me, Chendang," questioned Deckie, "what do your witch doctors say about that?"

Both children looked at the familiar sight without

surprise. It was a common thing to cut such a root when one was digging. "The soul of a chief has gone into it," said Chendang.

"Just as I expected," Deckie remarked. "Why God ever allowed such a plant to grow in this superstitious country, I don't know; but you two come over here to the medicine house, and I will tell you what will become of your souls."

Deckie drew the two children into the inner porch at the back of the medicine house. He threw down a mat, and they all sat down.

"You are right to associate blood with souls," Deckie began; "I will tell you why. Jesus was nailed to a cross of wood by cruel men, not for anything wrong that He had done, but for our sins. His blood flowed there to save our souls. Every soul has been bought by the blood of Jesus."

"The cross! The cross! 'He died on the cross to save us from sin.' That's what the song says!" Cherawa leaned forward to look in Deckie's face. "Please, Teacher Deckie, tell us what it means!"

"Jesus never sinned, yet He was nailed to the cross for our wrongdoing. He died in place of us. Our souls were bought with His blood." The earnest face of Deckie glowed with enthusiasm. "That's what it means," he said with emphasis.

"But Jesus never heard of me or Chendang,"

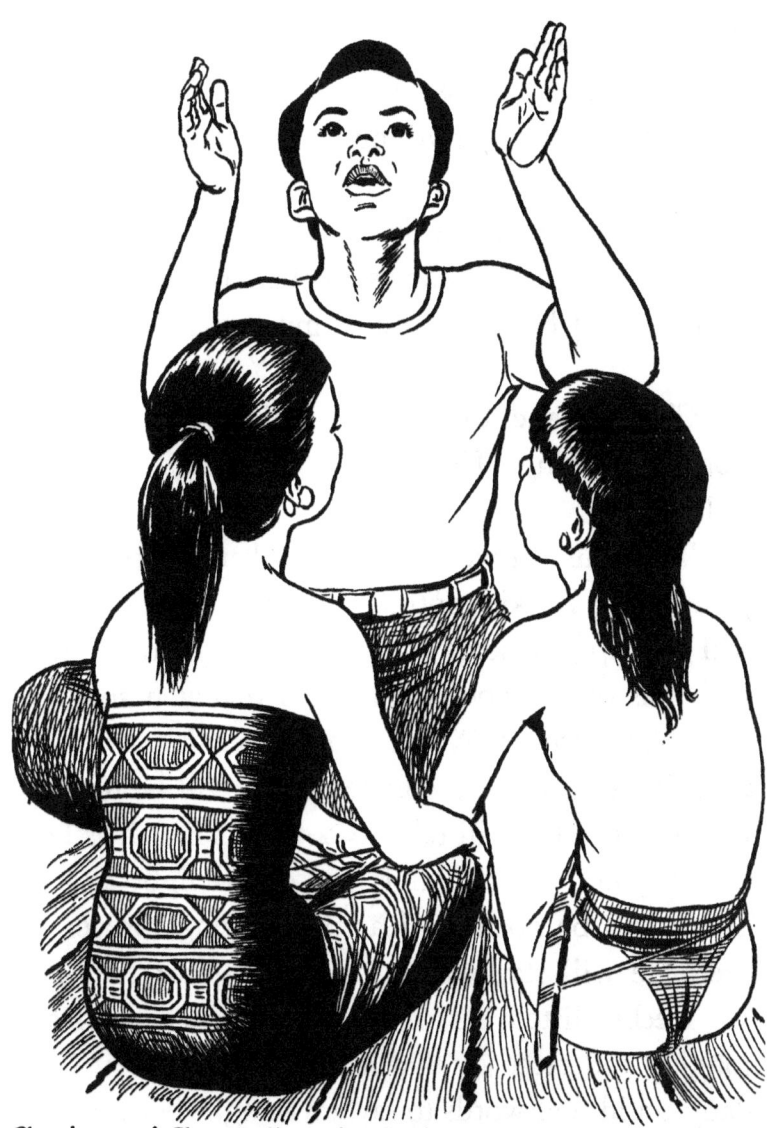
Chendang and Cherawa listened as Deckie told them about the Saviour.

Cherawa pressed. "How could He have died for us?" She must have the answer.

"Jesus knows everything. He knew everyone who would live on this earth from the very beginning, when He made it. He knows you better than your father or mother. He knows you better than you know yourself, and He loves you so much that He died for you."

Cherawa and Chendang sat thinking about this wonderful thing. They began to understand just a little.

"I promised I would tell you what will become of your souls," Deckie continued. "Don't think that Jesus will give up your souls easily after He has bought them with His own blood. He intends that you shall live with Him forever. When people die, that is not the end. Those who believe in Jesus and will be happy in His presence He will take to be with Him. It is beautiful beyond words. All is peace and light and joy. There will be no more fear or suffering forever and ever. He will stay with us always—Jesus Himself!"

Deckie lifted his face and looked up with such longing and utter joy that neither Cherawa nor Chendang could find words to say anything. They sat in the shade of the little porch and thought of what Deckie had said, and there arose a great tumult in the heart of Cherawa. She felt herself being swept along in a heavy current. It was like the time she was carried away in the flood. There was no way to turn back now. Her heart had gone out after this Jesus, this Man who had loved her so much He died to buy her soul from the power of the evil spirits.

"And what of those souls who refuse this Jesus Man?" Chendang at last found his tongue. "Where will they go?"

"They will have to be destroyed," Deckie said with sadness, "but none will ever be destroyed who love and follow Jesus."

Both children rose to depart. Deckie walked with them to their dugout. Chendang examined his basket of eggs. They were all right. No one had touched them. Then Chendang remembered.

"Teacher Deckie, Peekew has stolen the most powerful spirit charm known to the Ibans, and he intends to use it to drive you from this river, so be watchful." Chendang hung his head as he revealed this bad news, but Deckie did not appear to be greatly concerned.

"Bukit Nyala is under the protection of such great powers that Peekew's charms will not be able to prevail against it," Deckie answered with confidence. Then, seeing Cherawa's downcast face, he added: "But we will be watchful, and we will pray always. Will you not pray for us, too?" He addressed them both.

"Yes, teacher, I pray for you every morning and every night," Chendang replied, and Cherawa listened with amazement.

As they paddled with swift strokes across the river, Cherawa asked, "How do you pray, Chendang? Who taught you?"

"I asked Teacher Deckie long ago to teach me to pray. Would you like me to teach you?"

Cherawa thought for a long time. The current was swifter, the current that was bearing her toward Jesus. "Yes, Chendang, teach me."

"It is simple," he replied; "just think of Jesus until you can see Him in your mind. See Him all holy and clean and beautiful, His face so kind and full of love. See Him stand before you with both His hands outstretched to take you in; then just talk to Him like you would to your father." Chendang idled the oar he was holding. His face shone with the same light Cherawa had seen on the face of Deckie.

"I will do that," Cherawa said with simple grace.

The following day Chendang took his brown eggs to the garden that Dawee was already clearing for next year's rice field, and set them under one of the long-legged black fowls of the fighting-cock breed known in the river villages. There were eight eggs, and the little hen had difficulty in covering them all, but she at last tucked all eight under her wings.

Chendang protected the basket by fastening it to one of the supporting posts of the langkow, a simple roofed shelter always built at a garden spot. In his enthusiasm he built a pen for the baby chicks. It was late afternoon when he finished, and night had fallen when he tied his dugout to the home wharf.

He reported all his exploits to Cherawa. She had been eager to go along that morning, but Dawee had kept her home to help with the sago. The rice was gone now. Every family hunted what food they could find in the jungle. The sago offered the most nourishment for the least effort, so most of the villagers set out to gather it.

The thick porous lengths of the sago palm were grated over an open boat. Then the starch was washed free by stomping on the grated sago with the feet while fresh water was poured over it. The pure white starch was then placed in jars and covered with water to keep it moist. It rapidly soured. This did not diminish its nourishing qualities, but it tasted sour and rotten. Cherawa would rather starve than eat sago. Chendang brought fresh cucumbers from the garden for her, and she ate them with relish.

The next morning Cherawa and Chendang took a short trip to the mouth of Sungi Sap. It had been their intention to see for themselves again where the Naga had lain, and the horns on the sand; but at the mouth of the stream their courage failed them, and they crossed the river intending to pull upstream to Bukit Nyala. Then they saw the group on the sand bar. Peekew, Mapang, and Chief Rayang sat around the carcass of a freshly killed pig. Mapang had singed the coarse hair from the animal, and the three men were cutting off thick slices of the raw meat and eating it with evident pleasure. Mapang was quick to offer slabs of the dripping flesh to the two children. To the astonishment of all three men, they both refused.

"What is the reason you will not eat?" the chief inquired in surprise.

"We are not yet hungry," Chendang said with simple truth. They drew the dugout away from the sand bar and proceeded up river.

"Why would you not eat?" Cherawa asked her brother when they had rounded the curve and were approaching the tuan's village.

"I don't know," said Chendang; "I used to love nothing better than such a feast. Just now when I saw them there, with that bloody meat in their hands dripping all over their chests, I felt kind of sick. What about you?"

"I can't imagine Deckie or the tuan sitting there eating raw pig meat. I can't imagine Jesus doing it. That must be why we felt sick. Our hearts have gone out to follow Jesus, and we have to be clean like Him."

CHAPTER TWELVE

PEEKEW—HIS VICTORY

"I SUPPOSE a few well-chosen gifts and a small tribute paid to this witch doctor would quiet his objections," Deckie said to the tuan as they were discussing Peekew and his growing opposition.

"It might do so," answered the tuan, "but it would forever ruin our chances of winning him to Jesus."

"You are right," agreed Deckie; "we cannot give gifts until the people have discovered the real Gift we came to this river to bring. Otherwise we shall have a lot of followers who seek only selfish gain."

"And Peekew is so hard to touch! He has no wife and no children. He lives a solitary life all to himself. It is hard to find ways to be kind to him." Deckie turned the matter over in his mind while the two men unpacked a case of medicine and stowed it away behind the counter in the medicine house.

Cherawa and Chendang had just brought news of Peekew's latest plans. It was this that had started the conversation between the tuan and Deckie.

Through their peepholes the children had discovered Peekew preparing the material to lay a terrible curse on all the buildings at Bukit Nyala. When the bones and hairs and sticks were buried in the vicinity of the buildings, they would become unfit for human habitation. Perhaps they would burn down. Perhaps the people living in them would get sick. Or maybe the evil spirits would come in great numbers to possess the place. At any rate, it was the first measure to take to drive away the Jesus teaching.

Mapang had objected a little. He sat with Peekew as the old man prepared his charms. "I don't think the curses will do any good," Mapang stated in a discouraged voice; "I think the tuan has a charm against all our curses. Do you remember how I laid a curse on the knives I sold them? That was a long time ago, and none of their knives have given them any trouble."

"I believe Rayang is a follower of this new teaching in his heart." Peekew scowled at the bone he was whittling.

"Ever since you took Cherawa's galeega, the chief has been parted from you in heart," Mapang agreed.

"Stupid fool!" Peekew snorted. "That smirking Deckie has got on friendly terms with the chief's son."

"Remember, the chief has but one son," Mapang reminded him. "After all, the tuan and Deckie probably saved Chendang's life."

The two men sat and chewed so long on their quids of betel nut that the two listeners in the vacant room became weary and wished to depart, but such quiet prevailed that they feared to make a step lest they be discovered. It was early evening, but already dark. The two children squatted on their heels until they heard the door of Peekew's room open. The room was empty. The two men had gone.

Then they scampered out the seldom-opened door and stood leaning on the rail of the outer porch. They talked in whispers for a long time.

A boat was loosened from the wharf and paddled away toward Bukit Nyala. Was it Peekew and Mapang crossing over in the dark night to lay the curses? "It could be," Chendang thought out loud; "I suppose that is just what they are doing."

"And everyone over there is asleep now," said Cherawa. "They work so hard during the day. I'm sure they were in bed a couple hours ago."

"It will be an easy matter to bury the stuff near the buildings without being discovered. This tuan sleeps hard, and he does not lock his door." Chendang was worried.

Cherawa and Chendang then resolved to go early

in the morning to inform the tuan and Deckie of Peekew's secret doings and to discover, if possible, any traces of the curse.

The next morning they all stood in the medicine house. The tuan and Deckie were unpacking the medicine. Cherawa and Chendang had told the whole story, and they leaned now on the counter and watched the two men working. When the medicine was all put away, all four of them came down the steps and searched the ground around the medicine house. A light rain had fallen in the early dawn, but the sharp eyes of Chendang found a place where the earth had been disturbed. Deckie fell on his knees and, using the knife he always carried at his belt, soon uncovered the charms that were buried with great care and with evil hope.

Cherawa trembled as Deckie lifted the charms and held them out for tuan's inspection. Even Chendang took a couple steps backward. The terrible fear of the spirit charms was hard to throw off even yet.

"So this is what our friend is depending on to put a stop to the Jesus teaching!" The tuan regarded the handful of bones and sticks and hair with some amusement, but he did not laugh or make light of the matter.

"It is quite likely that the witch doctor may give some assistance to his charms, Deckie." The tuan was sober now. "We must be watchful."

It was almost time for the eggs under Chendang's hen to hatch. He had gone every day to the garden to see that the black hen had food and water. Then, just as the great day came, Jeria's mother had the dream. It was late in the night when her piercing scream rent the quiet air. A second scream followed, and by the time the third was heard, every inhabitant of Rayang's village was racing toward the center of the inner veranda.

Jeria's mother was dragged from her mat and sat trembling on the porch in the midst of her fellow villagers. Some of the women were screaming in terror. Everyone was afraid. Cherawa and Chendang, roused from sound sleep, clutched at their pounding hearts.

"What is wrong with you?" demanded Rayang in a loud voice. "What are you screaming about?" He shook the trembling woman by the shoulder. "Tell us at once!"

"The dream! The dream!" shrieked Indai Jeria. "Ayoh, ayoh, the terrible dream!"

At this, fresh screaming and sobbing broke out among the women. The faces of the men shone pale in the light of Nagal's candle.

"Tell us at once," commanded the chief, trying to make his voice steady; "everyone, be quiet! Indai Jeria will tell her dream."

"His head! His head!" she screamed. "It lay all bloody under the knife."

The wild-eyed woman stood up and, gesturing in the most dramatic manner, unfolded the terrible revelation: "It was a great knife! a great knife! It came down slowly and cut off his head." She covered her eyes to shut out the awful sight so vivid to her senses.

"Whose head?" screamed the chief and Peekew and Mapang and several others. Mapang put his hand under her elbow to keep her from falling.

"Whose head was cut off?" everyone wanted to know.

The distraught woman searched the assembled company until her burning eyes rested on Chendang. She pointed and took two quick steps toward him. "His head! His head!" she screamed. "It lay all bloody under the knife!"

Rayang turned pale. He dropped to his knees beside Indai Jeria. Dawee's wailing and sobbing rose to almost the same level as the dreamer's.

Peekew and Mapang exchanged knowing glances. Then the calm voice of Peekew spoke. "It is a warning, a warning," he comforted them; "if Chendang will stay in the village and not go out, the curse will probably be averted."

Cherawa had thrown herself on the bamboo floor of the porch and was sobbing and crying as if her own head already lay under the knife. Chendang touched her. His hand was warm and steady. "Don't take on like this, Cherawa; I am not afraid of their dreams and curses."

One by one the frightened people returned to their disturbed rest. Few slept any more that night. Next morning little else was discussed. The terrible fate of the chief's son was talked of on every hand.

"The boy has become much too friendly with the Jesus teacher across the river. The spirits must be very angry about it." Indai Mapang expressed her opinion.

"Surely, now, the chief will forbid the boy to go any more to Bukit Nyala. There is no more need for him to go. His wound is all well, and his ringworm is gone," another woman put in.

"Oh, by all means he should not be allowed to go for a full moon of days," one of the men ventured.

"He should never be allowed to go there any more! I'm sure it is a warning that the Jesus teaching will be like a knife to cut all our heads off," another replied with energy.

Peekew was in fine spirits that morning. He walked around among the excited villagers and said nothing, but he often rubbed his hands together with that little satisfied gesture so characteristic of him. It was evident that Indai Jeria had produced the dream at exactly the right time to suit his purpose.

When Chendang had finished his breakfast of the ill-smelling sago, and Cherawa had nibbled the end off a cucumber, Chendang took his paddle from the wall. His mother sprang upon him in terror. "No! No! Chendang, you shall not leave this room today!"

Chendang put her gently aside. "Mother,"—he ran his hand up and down the smooth edge of his paddle as he talked—"this is a test. This is a test to see whether I really love Jesus and trust Him. I don't fear the curses of dreams and charms any more. The evil spirits do not frighten me. My hen will hatch her eggs today, and I must go and care for her. Don't worry; Jesus will care for me."

As Dawee stood trembling under her son's hand, too astonished to speak, Cherawa spoke, "If you go, I will go with you." Snatching her paddle from the wall, she left with Chendang.

Before the startled villagers could collect their wits, the two children ran down the notched log, untied their dugout, and were paddling upstream.

"Look, Chendang," Cherawa said as she pointed back at the village, "they are all horrified at what you are doing! Do you think it is safe to insult the spirits like this?"

Chendang looked back at the row of excited people lining the porch rail of the outer veranda of his home village. Peekew was among them, gesturing with both hands. His meaning was clear. He commanded them to turn back at once.

Rayang was not there. He had crossed the river to Bukit Nyala early in the morning. Cherawa knew where he had gone, and marveled in her heart that he had done so.

Had Rayang been home, it is probable he would have set off in his own boat and brought his son back home by force; but no one else in the village, not even Mapang, had enough authority to cross the will of Chendang when his father was absent. So Cherawa and Chendang continued on up the river in the fresh morning with mingled feelings of fear and relief.

The garden clearing was not next to the riverbank. It was necessary to walk some distance into the jungle after mooring the dugout at the river's edge. The path was narrow and led between giant old trees of ironwood, too large and difficult to fell. So this bit of virgin forest had stood there for hundreds of years, undisturbed save for the runways the Ibans cut through the undergrowth beneath the great trees. The path led to a stretch of swampland farther back. It was here, in the edge of the swamp, that Dawee had chosen to clear a place for next season's planting.

A shelter stood in the edge of the clearing. It consisted of six sturdy tree trunks set in the ground like posts with a platform built up on them about six feet from the ground. There was a roof and a wall on the two sides facing the prevailing winds. It was under the shelter that Chendang had set his hen. The basket was tied to one of the supporting posts with thongs of rattan.

"I hear cheeping." Chendang laughed in great excitement as the two bent over the black hen's basket.

"Oh, look!" Cherawa touched a yellow head which had appeared among the black feathers of the mother hen.

With gentle hands Chendang lifted the black hen and revealed six enormous yellow chicks. He knelt with the mother hen in his arms and adored them like a devotee at a shrine. "Did you ever see anything like it!" Cherawa exclaimed. "Did Deckie say they came from somewhere over the sea?"

"They came from a country called America," Chendang informed his sister, with pride consuming him. "Deckie says they are named for one of the places in that great country. It is Rode Iland, or something that sounds like that."

"Will they be red when they grow up?" Cherawa asked.

"They will be just like the hens at the tuan's house," Chendang answered as he examined the two unhatched eggs. "These eggs feel heavy, and they have sounds." He held one and then the other to his ear. "I think these will come out, too. We will put the hen back on the basket and wait for a while."

So the two children spent the day at the shelter. They lunched on fresh cucumbers and discovered a palm stump which yielded a few tasty yellow grubs. It was enough. Their hearts were light. Later they noticed that the two remaining chicks hatched out. Chendang moved them to a clean basket, making them snug for the night.

To the great surprise of the children, no visitors came to disturb them, although they had made no secret of where they were going. No one appeared to persuade them back to the village. An ominous fear began to form in the heart of Cherawa. This was the worst defiance of the spirits that had ever been known on the river. It was not possible to disregard an evil omen like last night's dream without incurring the fierce wrath of all the dark powers.

"Chendang," Cherawa said as she laid a smooth brown hand on her brother's arm, "I am afraid."

"Then we will pray," Chendang replied. "Deckie taught me a word from Tuan Allah's book. It says, 'What time I am afraid, I will trust in Thee.'"

So together they knelt on the floor of the shelter and talked to Jesus. Chendang assured his sister that Jesus was actually there with them although they couldn't see Him. Then he prayed: "You know about the anger of the evil spirits, Jesus. You know about Peekew's charms and the dream of Indai Jeria. Cherawa is afraid. Take care of us, Jesus. How we love You! How we love You!"

Cherawa's prayer was as simple as her brother's. Comforted, they started down the path to the riverbank and their dugout. Chendang walked ahead with his paddle over one shoulder.

A few hundred yards from the riverbank a rending noise paralyzed both children. They halted in their tracks. A giant limb of an ironwood tree crashed to the ground. It fell so close in front of Chendang that he fell across it in weak fright. Cherawa screamed, but Chendang was laughing. "It didn't touch me!" he exclaimed in wonder. "God has sent His angel to keep me back just one step!"

Again the two children knelt by the fallen limb and poured out their young hearts in praises to Jesus. Then, scrambling over the barrier, they reached the dugout and paddled downstream in the fading light of sunset.

Cherawa looked at her brother as they approached the home wharf. His face was strangely flushed. Had he really been unhurt by the falling limb? Her heart gave a quick, sickening throb. He had not said a word since the prayer by the fallen limb. Cherawa made the dugout fast to the wharf. Then she took his arm and helped him out of the boat. "Come, Chendang, you are sick. I will take you to mother."

CHAPTER THIRTEEN

JESUS IS MY GALEEGA

ALL that night Chendang lay delirious on his mat. His face was scarlet. His eyes were bloodshot. He begged for water and mumbled constantly the name of Jesus and the name of Deckie. Rayang and Dawee hung over him in an agony of fear. He had defied the spirits. He had crossed the omens and had disregarded the dream sent to warn him. There could be no hope for him now—no hope!

Cherawa lay on the floor at the foot of Chendang's mat and wept aloud. Of what use were the prayers so trustingly spoken yesterday? Of what use were the light, joyous feelings that had possessed them both on the defiant trip to the garden? Her bitter tears fell all through the night.

It was of no use at all, of course. Then Peekew appeared at the door. "Let me come in, my friends; I will see what can be done for the strongheaded boy.

I have the galeega, you know. It is a powerful charm. Let us see what we can do."

Since no one forbade him, Peekew came after a few minutes with all his valued charms and spread them out next to Chendang's mat.

"You understand," said Peekew, his gentle voice firm and decisive, "that if the spirits relent and spare his life, there is to be no more friendship with this Jesus teaching, no more running after this Deckie and his master, the tuan."

Rayang still sat with bowed head. He made no reply to the words of the witch doctor. But Chendang had opened his eyes and saw Peekew. He raised himself up on his elbow and looked over the charms spread out beside his bed. Then, before them all, Chendang rose to his feet, unsteady at first, his face flushed with fever.

"Take these things away!" he commanded in a voice that made Peekew sit back on his heels in surprise.

"I worship Jesus. I trust in Him. I know that all these enchantments are the works of the devil and his evil spirits. Take them away!"

As Chendang talked, his flushed face became suddenly pale. "You are under the curse of the spirits!" screamed Peekew, all out of patience. "You are about to die. The charms say you cannot live!"

"Take these things away!" Chendang shouted at the startled Peekew.

A slow smile spread over the face of Chendang. He took one step forward and laid his hand on Peekew's shoulder. "I shall not die but live!" The healthy color crept slowly over his face. "This heavy fever was sent on me just to prove to you that by the power of Jesus I can arise and walk out of this room as healthy as I was yesterday morning." Chendang raised his eyes to look upward. No one moved. No one spoke. When the boy looked again at Peekew, whose shoulder he still held fast, the witch doctor was trembling.

"And you, Peekew, Jesus wants you. He loves you. I am a sign to you that Jesus loves you and calls you now to forsake this unhappy life of evil you have followed so many years."

So saying Chendang, with the old spring in his step, a light in his eyes, and the glow of perfect health evident in every fiber of his body, stepped to the wall, took down his paddle, and in another minute was untying his dugout from the wharf. Cherawa watched in astonishment while he rowed toward Bukit Nyala.

This remarkable thing had been witnessed by several of the villagers. The word spread rapidly through the village that Chendang, by the power of Jesus, had again defied the spirits and the witch doctor's charms and was perfectly recovered from his terrible fever.

"But Peekew said he would die!" cried Indai Jeria. "Did not my dream prove it?"

Then Cherawa, in an accession of strength she had never known before, spoke out among her elders: "Jesus is on Chendang's side. He is more powerful than all the evil spirits."

"You, then, believe on this Jesus, also?" Mapang asked, not out of scorn, but with surprise. Mapang had observed all the happenings of the eventful morning and had said nothing until now.

"I believe," Cherawa said as she looked at him without fear. "I also believe on Jesus."

Mapang went into his own room and closed the door. Peekew got into his boat and left. He went down the river and was last seen rounding the curve of the river in the direction of Sungi Sap.

Rayang and Dawee, utterly exhausted with the agony of the last twelve hours, rested in their room. Cherawa was not tired. Her heart was singing. Her body was refreshed. She sought the room of Garyu and Treesa. She found them praying.

"This is the day of victory for Jesus!" exclaimed Garyu with radiant face as they sat together on the floor. Treesa was well again, and the little boy was running everywhere.

Cherawa felt again the perfect peace of this humble room in the long house. This time her own heart responded in full measure. "I am also a believer," she said in simple confession.

That was a day long to be remembered in the village of Rayang. Nobody was ever quite the same again. The wicked spirits that had enslaved the village people so long had suffered a signal defeat. They never regained power in the village of Rayang.

As days passed, the change became more and more evident. The faith of Chendang and his bold acknowledgment of it had broken the back of heathenism in his village.

"The tuan's house on the hill is almost finished," said Jeria to Cherawa one morning a few weeks later. "Let's go and see it."

Together the two girls paddled over to Bukit Nyala and climbed the hill. The beautiful house was not quite done. It still lacked the shingles on the roof. Great piles of hardwood shakes stood at the foot of the hill.

"How would you girls like a job of helping to carry these shakes up the hill?" Deckie accosted them as they reached the front porch of the new house. "We need about twenty people to carry them, so we can get them all to the top today." He smiled his most engaging smile.

Both girls were glad to join the company of carriers, mostly from their own village. It was tiring work, but they stuck to it until everyone was through and the shakes stood in neat piles at the top of the hill.

Each worker was given a choice of wages. Some wanted two bottles of kerosene. Some wanted two measures of salt, but the mother of Jeria and the mother of Mapang took their choice last. They both wanted cloth jackets. The tuan asked them to come to the medicine house. All the others followed. Perhaps they were a little sorry they had not asked for jackets, too.

"Now, Indai Jeria, what kind of jacket do you want?" asked the tuan. Indai Jeria stood up and gestured in excitement. "I want a black jacket made of Chinese cloth," she insisted.

"And you, Indai Mapang, what kind do you want?" The mother of Mapang had been strangely subdued lately. In fact the difference in her behavior was noticed from the time of Chendang's miraculous recovery. She lifted her eyes to the tuan's kind face. "Just a jacket," she said; "I guess you know better than I do what will be right for me."

"All right, you shall both have your wish. You have worked hard and have earned it. I have written on this slip of paper just what you want. When I go home tomorrow, I will give it to my wife, and she will send the jackets when I return."

All the way back home Cherawa could hear the

mother of Jeria talking about the fine jacket she was going to have. The Chinese cloth was coarse and black and stiff, but it was the best thing Indai Jeria had ever seen. She could conceive of no greater riches at the moment. Cherawa clutched her two measures of salt with satisfaction. It would be a nice treat for the family.

Then Cherawa remembered all the times she had brought home bags of salt and rice from Bukit Nyala. She remembered how, just after Chendang's marvelous experience, the tuan had said to her as she came into the medicine house one morning, "You are looking very thin, my little girl. Don't you eat?" Then her father, the chief, who had been with her, laughed as he told the tuan that Cherawa would eat nothing but cucumbers. "We have no more rice," he confided; "the rest of us eat sago, but not Cherawa. She will only eat cucumbers."

The tuan had looked grave. Then he had turned and filled a bag with rice from the bin behind the long counter. "Chief Rayang," he said as he handed the bag to father, "this is for Cherawa. See that she eats rice every day. When this is finished, come and get more. I will have rice for her until the new crop is ready."

Yes, Cherawa remembered now, sitting in her dugout. She had eaten the tuan's rice for weeks. Now it was time to harvest the new crop. It was a good crop, too. No omens had disturbed planting or harvesting.

The heart of Cherawa was filled with music, and she gave way to her feelings by singing in a high clear voice "Everybody Ought to Love Jesus."

It was three days later when the tuan returned. Everyone had seen the white launch in the river. Indai Jeria and Indai Mapang flew to their boat and hurried across the river to receive their jackets. Cherawa and Jeria followed.

Behind the counter of the medicine house the tuan unfolded the jacket of black Chinese cloth. It was exactly what Indai Jeria had ordered. Her delight was

great. Her dark eyes snapped, and she looked at everyone with an expression that said plainly, "I was clever to choose this. It is perfect!"

Then the tuan unfolded the other jacket. A chorus of exclamations broke from the crowd of onlookers. None of them had ever seen such cloth.

"It is for you, Indai Mapang. Did you not tell me to choose what kind of jacket would be right for you? Here it is."

Still the mother of Mapang hesitated. "It can't be for me. No chief on this river has anything so lovely!"

"Yes, it is for you," the tuan insisted. "Deckie, explain to her."

Deckie picked up the jacket with his radiant smile. "This is the way of it," he began, addressing the whole group. "Indai Jeria chose the best she knew, but Indai Mapang chose to let the tuan select whatever he thought was best. Maybe Indai Mapang thought the tuan might know something better than she had ever seen. So it has turned out that way. Look, this is meant to teach you all a lesson. When we let Jesus choose for us, we will always get something better than when we choose for ourselves."

After that things happened fast. The tuan declared that the time had come to build the teaching house and the worship house. They were both set down on the level land near the landing place, so they were easy to reach. Then a fine little house for Deckie and his family went up between the teaching house and the worship house.

On Tuan Allah's rest day the believers came to worship their God and sing His praises in the little church under the jungle trees. Rayang and his family were often there. Deckie and Nuri taught the newcomers all the lovely songs that had been heard in the river for weeks.

The big house on the hill was finished. The tuan had brought his wife and five children to Bukit Nyala. The wonders of the big house were talked of up and down the river. There was said to be a talking box. Cherawa went to see this marvel and sat with the tuan's children cross-legged on the floor in front of the box while it talked and sang.

Peekew investigated this box, but he could find nobody in it. "It is a kind of magic," he said; "I have never seen that kind of magic before."

Two of the tuan's daughters had hair the color of ripe rice fields, golden and glistening. Their skin was white, so white that Cherawa sometimes wet her finger and rubbed it on the arms of the little girls to see if the color would come off.

"I guess their mother paints them with white stuff every morning so they will look that way," Jeria had said.

At last it was known that the white color was natural and the golden hair just grew that way.

The tuan's other children were like their mother, whose eyes and hair were dark. They did not seem so strange. Cherawa took great pleasure in visiting Ruth, the tuan's oldest girl, who was about her own age. In a very short time Ruth and Cherawa were conversing in a manner entirely satisfactory to them both.

One day Peekew appeared at the mission house with a bundle in his hands. He squatted on the veranda and opened the parcel. Cherawa saw him. She and Ruth were perched on the rail of the porch. They watched him spread his charms on the veranda. Then he sat beside them, patiently waiting until the tuan should come up the hill from the medicine house.

"I have brought them to you," said the old man as the tuan stepped onto the wide porch; "I have no more use for them. I also am a believer in Jesus. The power of the evil spirits has passed from me. Jesus is stronger than they all."

The tuan knelt beside the witch doctor and placed one hand on his shoulder; with the other he lifted first one and another of the well-worn charms.

"There is one more, the greatest of them all," said Peekew; "it belongs to Cherawa. I should like to give it back to her now." He took from his loincloth a small, irregular stone and held it toward Cherawa.

She stepped back in surprise. "No, Peekew, give it to the tuan. I shall never want it any more. Jesus is my galeega."

"I have seen what the Jesus teaching has done on this river." The old man smiled, and his voice held a gentle note of music no one had heard before. "I fought it for months, but now I have opened my heart, and Jesus has cast out the devil. I have seen the people with their new skins. I have seen the peace in their eyes and heard the songs they sing. I will follow Jesus."

Deckie had heard something of what was going on up the hill, and he came now to look on the collection of Peekew's charms with wet eyes and a glad face.

"Let us sing," said Cherawa; "let us sing 'Everybody Ought to Love Jesus.'"

We invite you to view the complete
selection of titles we publish at:

www.TEACHServices.com

scan with your mobile
device to go directly
to our website

Please write or email us your praises, reactions, or
thoughts about this or any other book we publish at:

www.TEACHServices.com • (800) 367-1844

P.O. Box 954
Ringgold, GA 30736

Info@TEACHServices.com

TEACH Services, Inc., titles may be purchased in bulk for
educational, business, fund-raising, or sales promotional use.
For information, please e-mail:

BulkSales@TEACHServices.com

Finally if you are interested in seeing
your own book in print, please contact us at

publishing@TEACHServices.com

We would be happy to review your manuscript for free.

www.ingramcontent.com/pod-product-compliance
Lightning Source LLC
Chambersburg PA
CBHW070538170426
43200CB00011B/2466